Deeper challeng... ... ..., ...en when everything is NO... ... ...e worship is in danger of becoming a cl... ...per calls us to genuine worship that doesn't depend on our circumstances.

Barry Blair — Nashville producer, Grammy Nominee, Dove Award winner (Audio Adrenaline, Bleach, Addison Road)

Sinking Deeper is an honest look into the life of a Christ follower who passionately wants to worship Jesus, especially during the storms of life. Kevin takes us far beyond the boundaries of worship just being defined by music, to worship in which we pursue the character of Christ.

Andy Frank, Worship Pastor Christ Church of the Valley, Peoria, AZ

"In his book Sinking Deeper, Kevin humbly reminds the reader what true Worship is: a continual desire to be in the presence of a Living and Loving God. Whether your life is sailing through crystal calm waters or is being thrown about by stormy waves, Kevin shares personally and biblically that the only way to truly find peace is by Sinking Deeper. I highly encourage you to read this book."

Garrick Whited, Producer - KLove Radio Network, Sacramento, CA

"I have known Kevin Earnst as a talented songwriter and gifted musician for several years now. But with his first book, Sinking Deeper: The Art of Worship While Drowning, Kevin shows himself to be a great storyteller as well. From the intriguing title to the honest personal stories, this book drew me in and pulled me on to keep reading. Most of all, Deeper draws me deeper as a worshiper and a follower of Jesus. This book is transparent, humorous and real. I highly recommend it."

Dr. Ken Read, Professor of Music , Cincinnati Christian University, Cincinnati, OH

"Kevin's conversational approach blended with his understanding of Scripture makes this book accessible and practical. Be encouraged and strengthened by his writings."

Justin Miller- Worship Pastor at First Christian Church, Napa, CA

"From the heart of a great songwriter, Sinking Deeper is a personal testimony full of encouragement and timeless truths. Honest, funny and convincing, Kevin challenges me to be a more faithful, passionate worshipper."

Mike Frazier, Worship Pastor, Savannah Christian Church, Savannah, GA

"In the tradition of men like Job, Elijah, Jonah, and David, Kevin Earnst wrestles with the eternal question, "Why do God's people suffer?" He writes with passion about a topic that is relevant to hurting believers: how to praise God in the midst of pain. The image of "worship while drowning" is extremely pertinent to those in difficult situations and offers much relief, comfort, encouragement, and hope to those who read this book."

Dr. Les Hardin, Associate Professor of New Testament, Florida Christian College

Kevin's book *Sinking Deeper: The Art of Worship While Drowning* is a refreshingly honest; truly helpful; and at times humorous read for those who want to and/or need to spend time with the Lord. This book can be especially a great help to those who experience times that are fearful. It has examples from scripture of how the patriarchs overcame in severe trials and uses contemporary examples to illustrate important spiritual points. An important concept which is presented in *Sinking Deeper* is that "worship is a relationship with God". This is not a popular notion and many who shouldn't miss this – unfortunately miss this. This book is full of faith and encourages faith in God. *Sinking Deeper* is an expression of how truly big God is.

Rufus Harris, President-Red Letter Records, pastor-The Bridge Church, Pontiac, MI

"We recommend that you read this book if you want a deeper relationship with Christ. While there's no formula to the Christian life, you will learn encouraging truths from Kevin's personal example in these pages. This book will be a blessing to anyone that reads it."

Michael and Cassandra O'Connor, Chicago, IL

This book explodes the concept of worship out of the church building and into the course of everyday life, a life that is often messy and complicated yet full of potential when God is in the midst. Kevin brings you face to face with the critical needs for a deeper lifestyle of worship in order to not only survive but thrive through any situation by God's grace. His practical thoughts, relevant stories, powerful portions of the Psalms and challenging questions will allow you to sink deeper in hope and joy as a result of the amazing power of worship. A great resource for personal growth, small group studies and sermon series!

Andy Hanson, Executive Director of Christ In Youth (C.I.Y.) Joplin, MO

SINKING DEEPER

(THE ART OF WORSHIP WHILE DROWNING)

Kevin Earnst

iUniverse, Inc.
New York   Bloomington

Sinking Deeper
(The Art of Worship While Drowning)

iUniverse books may be ordered through booksellers or by contacting:

iUniverse
1663 Liberty Drive
Bloomington, IN 47403
www.iuniverse.com
1-800-Authors (1-800-288-4677)

ISBN: 978-1-4401-3105-9 (sc)
ISBN: 978-1-4401-3104-2 (ebook)

Printed in the United States of America

iUniverse rev. date: 4/7/2009

CONTENTS

THANK YOU'S

First of all let me thank my friends Michael & Cassandra O'Connor in the Chicago-land area who once they heard of my endeavor in this process supported the costs of getting this to the publisher. I will never be able to thank you guys enough. Many people will be blessed by your awesome gift. Thank You!

Second let me thank Kathy and all my family back East for supporting me in this project for the past 5 years. Thank you Corey and Ethan as well for continually asking "Dad when are you going to finish your book?" (There's nothing like being motivated by your kids everyday to get something done. Thanks guys!)

Last but not least let me thank my good friends in Michigan, my many friends across this country I keep in touch with regularly (thanks to Facebook) , and my home group here in Flagstaff who have encouraged me for quite a while now to make this happen. I hope these thoughts and verses are helpful to you all whatever life may surprise you with.

*This book is dedicated to my mom, Judy.
Through you, over these past few months, I
have been reminded again of why I wrote this
book. No matter what comes your way whether
something as simple as a bad hair day to something as complex as cancer God is still God,
He has a bigger plan and deserves our worship.
Your life is the perfect reminder of that concept and a
great example of someone sinking deeper into Jesus.*

WAIT ON GOD'S DIRECTION,

OPENLY ASK FOR HELP

REALIZE YOU ARE NOT IN CONTROL

SURRENDER YOUR PLAN FOR A BETTER ONE

HOPE IN GOD

IMITATE THE LIFESTYLE OF JESUS

PRAISE HIM CONTINUALLY

AUTHORS NOTES

(MY PERSONAL DISCLAIMER)

This Book Took A Ridiculously Long Time

I actually started writing this book back in the late months of 2004. I finished it sometime in 2006 and then it sat on my shelf and collected dust. For the next whole year, 2007, I spent thinking about what I wanted to do with it. Publish it, don't publish it, keep it just to read on a rainy day, use it to prop up the corner of my bed or just pretend like it never happened and deny any knowledge of any personal documents ("Book? What book? I know nothing. You talking to me?")

I had always wanted to write a book so I had and there it was. I however had no idea how long it would take and what in the world I was getting myself into. (It's hard to believe now that in high school and college that I considered a 5 page paper for a homework assignment a lot of work.) In 2008, I set a goal to get it finished and publish it for real. That didn't work. Finally here it is 2009, 5 years later, and you are holding it in your hands. Amazing. Mark that off the list. Write a book. Check. Now you too have a copy to read and to collect dust around your house or even to prop up your bed with for years to come.

This Book Has A Story behind it.

So why this topic? What was the motivation? What's the story behind the madness? That's the question a friend of mine in northern California asked after he read the original manuscript. "Maybe you should share with the readers why you wrote on this particular topic." He asked. So here it is. My inside story on the writing of this book.

As most everyone has experienced at one time or another I believe I was going through a "spell" where you think the world is out to get you. You know what I'm talking about. When your bank account is screwed up, nothing seems to be going according to plan, everything in life seems to be off its axis and when you're putting your contacts in it won't come off your finger. Also in my case, throw in the stress that comes along with working in Ministry. I have been part of a church setting since I was being carried in the womb. Countless times along the way I have dealt with stressful and painful circumstances not only with team members and church members but also staff situations. It happens. Sometimes you have to agree to disagree and work through it. Sometimes it also involves learning the true colors of people you thought you knew well.

The chaos always seems to come from all angles and as we all know it often comes all at the same time. So in the midst of all this instead of breaking into a paranoia, thinking that the world was out to get me or turning my back on God and the church I just started developing a new fresh approach to my daily Bible reading time and developing my creative gifts. I searched for scripture, I journaled about it and I wrote new songs. I finally had time that I had wanted for years to really focus on those creative gifts and time with God that I had missed out on, ironically even though I was working in a church.

Then it happened. Each day in some weird way I would find myself repeatedly coming across these key verses and thoughts. Someone would randomly say it in a conversation at a Restaurant,

Me: I'll take a number 3 and could you make that a Biggie Size?"

Cashier: "OK that $6.53 and did you know that if you know that if you trust God He will make your paths straight?"

I'd hear a song with the same words, Id get stuck behind a car with it written on a bumper sticker. I'd hear it as part of a long conversation waiting in a line. It would just happen to be the sermon topic at church that week or even said in passing on a TV show. It's as if it was being carefully planned out. Like some kind of conspiracy. For a while I thought I was on some weird reality show and Howie Mandel was going to pop out from behind the counter.

I remember one day specifically, I was sitting in a waiting room and all of the sudden in walked a guy with a T- Shirt on with a quote from a verse I had been studying that week and was journaling on that very morning. He walked by and of course just sat down in the seat next to me. I just sat there and gave him that mysterious stare. It took me a moment to get up the courage but I leaned over quietly and said "Excuse me... this might sound strange but did someone pay you to wear that?" He just smiled and looked at me as if I was just let out of the home. Not satisfied with that response and now on a role I asked another ice-breaking question or two. "Are you stalking me? Who told you to wear that? Is that your shirt? Who's watching this?" Suddenly security showed up with a tazer and all I remember was shouting out, "I can see you! I know you're watching!" and then I woke up a day later in a padded room.

Ok that last part isn't true and none of these questions got answered but we did have a good conversation about how ironic it was that his shirt happened to be the theme of my life for that week and how God works in mysterious ways. So for months...

even the next year I kept running into these verses that I read, journaled about and prayed over. Now here they are. The chapters that make up the book you are going to read. The songs I wrote are from the same verses and will be all part of my new CD "One Step Closer" out this summer. It's obvious God was speaking to me in a powerful way through words that not only I needed to hear but also many other people I have shared this with over the years and now you. I knew throughout the writing process that God was helping me grow and be stretched into something more. It all started from me making the decision on how to deal with those present "storms". I chose to turn it into something good.

Whether music or journaling, the creative outlet of writing is my way of connecting with God and so I kept focusing on my goal of writing no matter what the case and I hope you benefit from them as much as I did.

This Book is a Survival Guide.

We all need a survival guide. It's crazy out there. Along this journey we may sometimes find ourselves "lost at sea" and overwhelmed by life as we try to keep our heads above the water. We need some inspiration and encouragement. Everyone's been there before whatever situation you may have faced or be facing presently. It can literally feel like you're drowning. How do I know what drowning feels like? Well I don't but I can imagine it's pretty intense. So if you're dealing with some pretty tough stuff and feeling this way then this book was written just for you. If you are literally drowning and were mislead by the subtitle, I apologize. Let me just say that I wouldn't really recommend using this book as a guide in your present situation. Just try to keep your head above water and yell for help. Drop the book. You can get another copy later.

This Book is a Personal Testimony

This book is very much like a very long personal journal and since you paid for it I guess you can read it. Some of it is very, very deep and close to my heart. Other parts it seemed like God was clearly telling me to write. Some of it may seem like it was written off the top of my head after long periods of no sleep. Whatever the case, I can guarantee that every word written on every page was discovered through my own personal journey to improve my relationship with Jesus and my worship to Him. There are words and thoughts and scriptures that metaphorically became a lifeline for me while I felt like I was drowning and calling out to God. I long to worship God with my life even while in the midst of crisis or struggle and through this journaling process I was able to do just that. I pray you will be able to as well.

This Book is a Devotional/Scripture study

This book was written to be read on a daily basis. Let me re-word that. You don't have to read the whole thing on a daily basis. Just break it up and use it a little at a time. Make it a process and not a one- time event. Unless you want to read it daily, then go for it. It will be good for you. Read the devotional thoughts and scriptures. Think about them. Pray about them and apply them to your life. This process of studying has been around for ages and is guaranteed to work. Post the scriptures on your mirror, on your door, in your cubicle, or your office wall. Pray daily as you learn in your adventure. Whatever you do however, don't use this book as a replacement to Bible reading even though it does include scripture. That may be hard to explain to God when you see him someday face to face and I don't want my name brought up in that conversation.

This Book is a Form of Worship

No, this doesn't contain chord charts and sheet music to sing as praise and worship at your church, however it is all about worshipping our awesome Creator Jesus Christ. Worship as we know is more than singing just singing songs anyway. This book is about building a relationship. It's about building a deep relationship with Jesus. That is the focus of true worship. Developing a sincere relationship with our Almighty God. Through these thoughts and ideas you too can find yourself worshipping God no matter what comes your way. This book isn't just about how to survive the sea of pain, hurt, doubt and confusion but how to worship God while you are in that sea and trying to stay afloat.

Read. Pray. Grow.

Read through the questions included and journal your thoughts along the way. Let these thoughts and ideas encourage you on a daily basis. Sink deep into the heart of God while being lifted up closer to his presence in worship.

CHAPTER 1:

MAYDAY! MAYDAY!
(EVERYTHING'S ABOUT TO CHANGE)

It's not every Friday evening that I find myself with nothing to do. It's actually a pretty rare thing. There seems to always be something to do. However this particular Friday night I was in desperate need to take time, unwind and relax at home so I decided to do that by watching a movie. So there I was, meandering aimlessly around the local video store on a quiet Friday evening. I'd already been down every aisle a couple times and I was making my rounds again as if something this time was going to miraculously jump out at me and capture my attention. Nothing seemed to hit the spot. Classics, action adventure flicks, new releases, seen that, seen that, never want to see that, can't believe I've seen that. I was just about to settle for a re-run at home or maybe just swing next door for a Cappuccino at Starbucks when finally it finally caught my eye. There in a row on the top shelf was entire first season of the popular TV show *Lost*.

Now be aware at this time I had no idea what *Lost* was about. I had heard it was an awesome show but never before had I taken the time to catch an episode on the tube. Why not give it a try? I thought so I grabbed a copy and checked out. Two days later I found myself at the store buying the whole first season. I was hooked. I was officially a *Lost* addict. My life would never be the same.

I absolutely love that show! Even though I didn't get captured into this mysterious new series until after the first season I was guaranteed now to never miss an episode and religiously watch each one every Wednesday night. Any other addicted Lost fans out there? It's ok you can admit it. The first episode of course was pretty intense as this massive jetliner comes crashing down out of the sky and leaves a mess of debris and wounded passengers strung out all along the shoreline. It's in this episode the show introduces one of the main characters, we all know and love as Jack, played by Matthew Fox who tries to save the day.

Remember how the season started? His eyes opened wide as he slowly sat up and began to regain consciousness. His face was flooded with fear and confusion. What had happened? What's going on? What the first season really doesn't show at all is how the crash actually happened. Instead it gives you bits and pieces in flashbacks throughout the series. Minutes before this mass hysteria Jack and everyone on the beach were flying safe and sound high over the ocean headed from Australia to L.A. Just another day. Just another flight. Or so they thought. The view I'm sure was great looking out over the ocean, the clouds floating by and the sun rays breaking through. But that had all come to an abrupt ending as they now were finding themselves stranded in a mysterious place trying to fight for their lives. As the show progresses the passengers of flight are now setting up camp on the island and discovering new mysterious things in this new place they call home. Life changed in a matter of minutes and nothing would ever be the same.

What is so addicting about the show for me, other than the mystery of the island and the creativity of its producer J. J. Abrams, is that in some strange way I know many of its viewers, including myself, living in today's culture can relate to the whole idea of change, interruption, pain and sometimes being lost.

Being anywhere stranded or lost can be overwhelmingly stressful. Whether it's waiting at the airport waiting for that flight to get home, running out of gas out on the highway or being totally confused about some new life altering decision you need to make, it's always un-surprisingly stressful and frustrating to say the least. Not to mention your original plans or intentions have been changed and altered and no one likes unexpected changes. Especially if they're painful.

What is Going On?

It's not earth shattering news to announce that life itself is full of instant changes, unwanted interruptions and awkward surprises. Have you ever noticed that just when you least expect things like that to occur that's when it always happens? One minute the weather is sunny and beautiful, the next there's a storm. One day you're flying high and the next you've hit rock bottom. One minute you don't have a care in the world and life couldn't get any better, the next absolutely nothing seems to be going right and your world is caving in. Changes have a way of sneaking up on you like that. For instance, not too long ago on a Saturday morning I woke up and started off the morning watching cartoons with my kids. To our surprise shortly after, the power went out. Change of plans. "Not sure what's going on but I guess we're going to have to find something else to do." A small inconvenience for us. Just a few miles away a small plane had crashed into the local power supply and three people were killed. Change of plans. Life was interrupted.

We want to live life and have some control over what comes our way. We want to know what lies ahead so we can be ready to deal with it when it comes. In order to have some kind of normalcy, simplicity and order we try planning our own lives or maybe even keep a schedule. A schedule of things we want to happen or know are going to happen. Just log it in your daily planner or maybe your new high tech phone. That way you have it all under control. "Lunch next Thursday at 1? Let me see what I have, Ok yes I can squeeze you in then no problem."

We live by the beat. We follow a routine, a daily schedule and everyday are driven to try to be better at what we do, to try and get ahead in life and find our purpose and reach our goals. But along the journey we often find ourselves facing difficult situations, struggles, disappointments, tragedies, experiences, events that changes "life as we know it" and may even toss you "out of the boat" and send you out into an ocean of hurt, confusion and doubt. " What a death in the family? I'm being laid off work? "A 20 year old relationship has to come to an end? "Um. Let me check my planner again…. No… no… I'm sorry I'm completely booked. I can't fit that in right now. Get back with me in a couple months or better yet… never." If it were only that simple to avoid the pain. I heard of these kinds of things referred to as life-changing earthquakes and that is just what they are.

Will It Ever End?

The things we like the least in life such as tragedies or crisis are the things that seem to schedule themselves into our lives on their own. It's in these times that life loses its luster and we again not only find ourselves discovering the frailness of our humanity as we are forced to keep treading water to stay afloat. You know the experiences I'm referring to. These life-changing earthquakes are the challenges, transitions and difficulties in life that stretch us into something more. They take life and turn it inside out and upside down. Here are some you may be familiar with:

- A Death
- Moving to a different part of the country
- A career change
- Searching for purpose and meaning
- Making a major personal decision
- A job loss
- The news of bad health

- Fear of divorce
- Overwhelming Stress
- Financial crisis / a struggling economy or even
- The questioning of your faith.

The list goes on and on. Everyone has been there at one time. No one is immune to the pain. Young and old, short and tall, every culture, religion and color. If you haven't already had to face a life changing earthquake similar to the ones mentioned above, sorry to say but your times coming. It's a time where you come to a crossroads in your life and all the questions come to mind. Why? What just happened? What am I all about? Why is this happening? Where do I go from here? Is there more to life than this? Ever felt this way?

Change

No one wants change but everyone has to deal with it. No one wants to have their life interrupted in anyway and especially when it involves hurt and confusion but we all have to agree that no matter what it's going to happen. No one wants to be faced with big and overwhelming questions with no possible answers. But you have to understand that no matter how miserable it gets, there are answers beyond the unknown and one all-powerful creator who is in charge of every minute piece of creation. He's always around and knows the final outcome. If you really think you have it bad or have been through some pretty devastating challenges remind yourself of Job. You know the story. Imagine being this guy

"Have you considered my servant Job?" God said to Satan as Satan came before him

"There is no one on earth like him. He is blameless and upright. A man who fears God and shuns evil."

Now here is the ultimate story of change and interruption. Satan tries to use his power to completely destroy Job's character and integrity but God knows without a doubt in His mind that there is no way that will ever happen. Which is why he even brings up Job to Satan in the first place? (Imagine having such a deep faith that even God himself is impressed!) Chapter one of the book of Job goes on to tell this incredible story.

> *"One day when Job's sons and daughters were feasting and drinking wine at the oldest brothers house, a messenger came to him and said, "the oxen were plowing and the donkeys grazing nearby and the Sabeans attacked and carried them off. They put the servants to the sword and I am the only one who has escaped to tell you!" While he was still speaking, another messenger came and said, "The fire of god fell from the sky and burned up the sheep and the servants, and I am the only who has escaped to tell you! While he was still speaking, yet another messenger came and said, "The Chaldeans formed three raiding parties and swept down on your camels and carried them off. They put the servants to the sword and I am the only one who has escaped to tell you!"*

and if that wasn't enough already..........

> *"While he was still speaking yet another messenger came and said, "Your sons and daughters were feasting and drinking wine at the oldest brothers house, when suddenly a mighty wind swept in from the desert and struck the four corners of the house. It collapsed on them and they are dead."*

What words or thoughts could possibly come to mind after this amount of shock? Everything he had owned, loved and worked was now gone, instantly wiped off the face of the earth. All wealth and family was taken away in a matter of minutes. One life drastically changed in every possibly way in one un-forgetful afternoon. Luckily not everyone will experience such a tragedy.

Where is God?

The world itself has experienced such events that have brought a lot of change. Think about it. September 11th, the Tsunami in Asia of 2005, the Columbine High school shootings, the war in Iraq and so many others. We see it. We hear about it. We don't believe it and the questions start flooding our minds again. Why? What just happened? What is going on? What is the point? Where is all this leading to? Is there more to life than this? Life doesn't always work the way we want it. And it shouldn't because we aren't in charge! Life doesn't seem to really make a lot of sense. And it never will to us anyway. It often leaves us lost in limbo, hopeless, helpless, hurt and feeling like we're drowning in an ocean of despair. That's because we're human. The bottom line is we can't live without these feelings and difficulties. The real question is where do you think God is in the middle of all these heartaches and struggles?

We worship a God who is mysterious. He doesn't fit into our understanding of how things should be taken care of or formulas of common sense. God is not our magic genie. He is God. His ways are not our ways. Our expectations of God and who God really is are extremely different. Have you ever thought about that? All this time you might have been worshipping a God you imagined in your head when ultimately you are finding out who God really is more and more everyday. It might not make sense but he may be actually using your life changing earthquakes to do something new in your life.

Ever thought about that? Stop and ask yourself this. Do you believe that he could be working on you and through you as well as using you through these events? Why else would these things be happening anyway? Are you able step beyond the changes and find ways to worship Him even when life makes absolutely no sense? Does the fact that God is ultimately in control of it all make things look a little clearer for you? Or maybe even cause you to be a little more relaxed about what may happen tomorrow?

What is This All About?

So what is it that is bringing a major interruption to your life right now? Are you possibly going through a time of transition, a time of searching for answers and personal struggles? Maybe you are at a time in your life where you are trying to strengthen your faith and rebuild your passion. Or maybe you just like any of the rest of us need some insight and encouragement to go deeper into the love of Jesus. If so then this book is for you. That's what this is all about. You are on a journey. A spiritual journey. These thoughts and scriptures are things I've learned to understand along the way along my journey as well. They are helpful tools and insight to remind yourself of when you feel like your drowning in all the change. If you are spiritually drowning my prayer is that this will help you along as you search to find your way back to shore and as you try to worship in the pain. Then hopefully you too can help someone else.

So you read the story. What do you think you would do if you were Job? Realistically now. I'm not sure what I would be able to do or say. I only hope I would have the passion he had. The passion and strength to shout out in the middle of a crisis with nothing but praise for our God. That is pretty intense! What kinds of words come to mind when you face a crisis? Better yet what words flow out of your mouth in times like these? Job lost his family and wealth in a short time frame and this is his reply......

> *The Lord gives and the Lord takes away, may the name of the Lord be praised!!'*

This guy was obviously passionate about his God no matter what came his way.

Worship in the Chaos

I'm sure those around him must have thought he had snapped and mentally checked out under the shock of it all. Every way you look at it though, it's obvious that this one of a kind individual was close to the heart of God. Was this experience tragic and painful for Job? Yes. Did Job grieve through his loss? Of course. Did he grow even closer to God through this experience? Closer than a lot of us today could ever imagine. The point is though that Job found a way to worship God while even in the middle of such heartache and transition. That's not something many people can do or have even ever thought of. Worship God in the middle of your darkest hour? Right when you most feel the furthest away from anything and anyone? Yes. That's when you really, truly can diagnose how close to God you really are. That's when it really matters the most.

Worship is all about showing worth to something that we think is valuable. Job found value in his relationship with God and exhibited that value in his darkest hour. Worship is about a relationship with God. A relationship that lasts through any sunny day or storm that we may encounter. Worship is easy to do when you're excited and all is well. What about when life has drained you of all you have, kicked you down and left you stranded? Or when all your passion is gone and you are filled with frustration and confusion. Do you think you would still find yourself having that drive and ambition to praise with all you've got? Chances are probably not. This is exactly what I'm talking about. This is the moment when you begin to understand a whole new level of worship. It's heartfelt worship offered when you feel you have nothing left to give.

We need to worship when there is an enormous void to fill. We need to worship when we are lost and in the midst of any kind of struggle. God is still God, deserving and worthy of our praise even when you are in a hard place and have nothing. I made for myself an acrostic of the word worship to remember when times are hard and I still need to worship. You may think word acrostics are over- rated but I have found this to be very helpful to remember all these different point. Here is what I came up with and will use throughout the book.

- W Wait on God's direction *(It just may become your new hobby)*
- O Openly ask for help *(Cry, yell, scream, etc, etc)*
- R Realize you are not in control *(I don't have a clue)*
- S Surrender your plan for a better one *(Give it up)*

- H Hope in God *(There is a way out)*
- I Imitate the lifestyle of Jesus *(what better role model could you ask for?)*
- P Praise Him Continually *(in the good, bad and the ugly)*

How Deep Can You Go?

Max Lucado told part of this story in one his books I have in my collection. It interested me so I researched this story a little deeper and found out some more interesting facts and details. Pipin Ferraras is a Cuban deep sea diver who set the worlds record for the furthest free dive. With just flippers and a wet suit for about three minutes and twelve seconds this daredevil dropped nearly the depth of a 55 story building and went a record-breaking 531 feet below the surface of the ocean! This story was reported worldwide and was logged in the Guinness World Record for free-diving. This is an amazing story of will power and human skill but it's not the end of the story.

On October 12, 2002 an even more ambitious diver named Audrey Mestre, who just happened to be Pipin's wife decided to break the record and try for 561 feet. This world class athlete on a single gulp of air wrapped around a weighted sled began to descend to meet her goal. While diving to this kind of ocean level the story is that divers " withstand near crippling water pressure, their lungs shrink to the size of baseballs, their heart slow to 20 beats a minute and their sinus cavities fill with salt war to keep their eardrums from exploding." But then as she began to reach the final mark a tragedy occurred. Rough water on the surface caused the cable she was coming back up on to bend and as she began to come back up she did not ascend quickly enough. On the way back to the surface she lost consciousness and after being rescued she was already dead after being underwater for 8 minutes and 48 seconds which was more than 5 minutes past her maximum ability.

How Deep Are You Willing To Go?

If only we had that kind of drive and ambition to go deeper into the heart of God and to get closer than anyone ever has. How awesome it would be to have a passion to know Him better than a close family member or best friend. Audrey died while trying to set a deep free diving record. What are you willing to die for? Better yet what are willing to live for? Growing closer to your personal Creator is going to be challenging and maybe even painful but don't you think it will be worth it in the end? Even more than being remembered for setting a world record? Do you think you would notice if an opportunity to know God better stared you in the face? Do you think you would take the chance? Would you believe me if I told you that your personal crisis, change, struggle, heartache whatever the case may be might just be the open door to do just that? Or that it might actually be the reason why you are in the place that you are right now in your life?

Here's another question. Is your relationship with God right now strong enough where you can continue worshipping Him even if your change might be incredible painful? If not then maybe this is your chance to learn how to exalt God as Job did through the good and the bad. Don't think you will be able to save yourself even if you think you have the full ability to do so. You will just find yourself treading water a little longer. Don't think there is any lifeboat or raft coming in a hurry to your rescue. It might not be on the way. It's not always that easy and most of all it might not be part of God's plan. All may seem hopeless and you may feel like you just took your last gasp of air but don't be overwhelmed. You may have been tossed overboard and feeling like your lost at sea or come crashing down out of the sky but maybe it's exactly where you're supposed to be. You may think your drowning when really all that's happening is an opportunity to go deeper into the heart of God. After all God promised in all things He will make good. So maybe your changes are a step in a better direction.

CHAPTER 2:

CAN YOU HEAR ME NOW?

(SILENCE LOUDER THAN WAVES)

"In my distress I called to the Lord and he answered me. From the depths of the grave I called for help, and you listened to my cry. You hurled me into the deep, into the very heart of the seas, and the currents swirled about me. All your waves and breakers swept over me. I said I have been banished from your sight, yet I will look again toward Your holy temple. The engulfing waters threatened me the deep surrounded me, seaweed was wrapped around my head. To the roots of the mountains I sank down. The earth beneath barred me in forever. But you brought my life up from the pit O lord my God. When my life was ebbing away, I remembered you Lord and my prayer rose to You. What I have vowed I will make good. Salvation comes from the Lord."

Sounds like another wonderfully crafted lyric from the popular Psalmist right? Wrong. These are heartfelt words from a man soaking in stomach acid from head to toe, surrounded by darkness, smelling like intestinal odor and floating possibly hundreds of feet below the surface of the ocean. Not a great situation to be in but it's true. This is the prayer of the man we know as Jonah. If anyone had a reason to be crying out for help he was the one. I've heard of people swallowed whole by alligators or literally bitten in half by sharks but not very often does anyone live to tell about it. Let alone pray with such depth and passion while it's happening.

The Call For Help

If you were swallowed by a whale and needed help what would you do? As crazy as it may sound I think I would try using my cell phone. Maybe you could make a call or text for help. The problem is with my bad reception the odds of getting a signal in the internal organs of a whale in the bottom of the ocean would probably be not so good. Considering my calls gets dropped while I'm on my phone kicked back on the couch. Even if you did get a hold of anyone up there who is going to believe you anyway. I imagine this would be the sort of call even 911 operators would be doubtful of and maybe even classify as "most un-believable call of the year". Whatever the case what would you do? What other options would there be? Other than making a call here are some other options I came up with.

A. Try being brave and craw back out.

B. Convince him of how many fat calories you are hoping he spits you out.

C. Face the fact that it's all over.

D. Pray hard to be rescued any other way than the way you're about to experience.

Jonah picked option D. In the midst of his worst moment as vulgar as it probably was He called out to God. God in all His splendor hears the prayer as He always does (no matter where they are coming from) and answers. Check that verse out again. It says right there in the story "God heard and commanded the fish to spit him out." What an awesome God. That beats any phone network I've ever heard of, not to mention any normal way a giant fish may remove you from his stomach.

The Official Cry For Help

S.O.S   You've probably heard these letters together before. They are the international Morse Code distress signal. This code consists of three dots, three dashes and three more dots (...---...) These letters when first designed not as an abbreviation but were just were put together as the simplest form of communicating when in extreme need of help. Made for even an amateur radio operator. Later on users made the S.O.S. into the phrase "Save our Ship" and even my favorite, "Save Our Souls". The first real use of the SOS code was during the sinking a ship on April 15, 1912 we remember today as the Titanic. In all reality Jonah sent out an S.O.S. in his time of need. In a time like that all you really can do is pray and cry for help. In Jonah's case that's exactly what it took to be rescued.

S.O.S from the Psalms

King David often prayed similar prayers as the one Jonah did as he found himself going through personal struggles throughout his entire life. We think of his writings in the Psalms to be songs of praise, worship and thanksgiving when the real truth is that over a majority of the Psalms are songs crying out to God in a time of need. Also called a Lament.   For example,

> *"Save me O God, for the waters have come up to my neck. I sink in the miry depths, where there is no foothold. I have come into the deep waters, the floods engulf me. I am worn out calling for help. My throat is parched." Psalm 69 and even this one. "O Lord the God who saves me, day and night I cry out before you. May my prayer come before you turn your ear to my cry. Psalm 88.*

14

Skim through for yourself and you will find dozens of heartfelt prayers from David as he searched for God through difficulty. I have found many of the Psalms to be not only comforting but sometimes even word for word how I have felt at one time or another. Tragedy and transition often has that effect on us. Somehow it makes us all of the sudden remember there's a God out there and we find ourselves again praying and searching for answers. God help me! I need your hope. I am lost and confused. Show me the way. What do I do? What happens next? Where are you leading me?

Worship in the Good, the Bad and the Ugly

Whatever the situation may be prayer helps us to again reconnect with God and get back on track. It also helps to find peace while dealing with heartache. It is so easy to worship God and focus on Him when times are good, when things are going our way and any sign of problems are far from sight. But when someone starts making waves that's when we get uneasy and we start to panic. Suddenly the present and future seems unclear and unhopeful. When tragic change occurs then we find ourselves back on our knees begging for things to be back to normal again. We call on God to bring answers but rarely come before Him in relentless worship for all He is regardless of where we are stuck. We just want a way out of our dilemma. We only want resolve. We lack trust.

I keep thinking of a scene from the movie "O Brother Where Art Thou." The three southern bandits in the movie find themselves again up between a rock and a hard place as they come to face to face with the law who want to hang them on the spot for "getting in their way of doing things". George Clooney who plays the leader in the pack then drops to his knees and pours out a desperate cry for God in his deep southern drawl. He asks for wisdom, he asks to be saved and asks for any way of escape and in return he will be baptized, become a better religious man and never ask for anything again.

Suddenly the answer to his prayer came as a flood like tidal wave hits and the rivers rise washing away everyone and everything sending them floating down through the town on debris. Clooney soon enough pulls himself to safety and is afloat with his fellow con team and in a quick response chalks the whole thing up to sheer coincidence and carries on with life as before.

Worshipping God when things are good is easy. Worshipping God when things are hard shows how deep our love for worshipping God really is. Finding something to praise God about when in a dilemma is what truly defines what we think of God himself. When in need we beg for help. We show our lack of trust in what God can do and don't celebrate Him for all He has already done. What we need to do is call on Him in prayer and know He will take care of all needs as we put all selfish agendas aside.

Worship, to make it simple is the act of showing worth to something or putting our focus and attention on one thing. So even prayer itself is one way of worshipping God. Praying to God shows that we recognize His presence. Prayer shows that are open to His will and He is willing to make that known if we only worship Him. God deserves to be worshipped and exalted in the good and the bad. No matter what the circumstance, God is still God. Calling on Him, recognizing who He is and what He can do, can not only provide answers through the hardship but also allows us to give Him glory as we go through it. With God there is no doubt that you will sooner or later make sense of it all. All you have to do is call. S.O.S, ...---... No need to even use the speed dial. No bad signal. No roaming fees. He's always ready to listen and help. Let me explain about the uniqueness of God....

Omnipresence: Everywhere

Omni who what huh? It may sound scientific but it's really just a fancy word meaning God is everywhere all the time. Don't ask me to explain it in scientific detail or theological jargon. It's just that way. What it means for us though is that no matter where we are at whatever time God is there too. In your living room, God is there. On the job, God is there. At your favorite restaurant, God is there. From the vastness of space to the bottom of the ocean You are guaranteed God is present. From Sandusky, Ohio to the foothills of Tibet. To make it even more complicated while He's in Sandusky, He's also in Tibet at the same time and in the bottom of the ocean and in space. It kind of puts a whole different spin on things doesn't it? We have no logical excuse why we can't call on God anywhere, anytime. Calling on Him wherever we are gives God glory as we recognize he is always available. "Can you hear me now? Good"

Omnipotent-Powerful

Calling on God shows that we know He has the power to help us. And of course He does. He's God. Hollywood has made a killing on movies about people with power. Superheroes grace the big screen and our TVs constantly and are always saving anyone who needs there help and find themselves in a situation where they feel powerless. Batman, Spiderman, the Incredible Hulk, X-Men. We all love those characters. After all everyone needs a hero don't they? It's pretty cool to think if you are stuck in a burning building Spiderman can come swinging in and bring you to safety or if there is a world-wide disaster taking place Superman can fly around the world causing it to change orbit and turn backwards to make up for a little loss time. Man in all his unique design created Superheroes… God created man…. Need I say more? Think about it.

God is powerfully amazing and amazingly powerful.

Omniscient-Smart

Last but not least calling on God shows that we understand God can provide knowledge and answers in our time of need. Isn't it funny that in a time of need sinner or saint alike we find ourselves naturally in prayer calling on a "higher power"? We are created in the image of God to be full of knowledge and wisdom and even at the end of the rope we have a natural instinct to ask God himself for insight. It's the way we are wired. We don't understand it so maybe God will. We live in an information age with the world-wide web, computers, literature, media, and advanced education but literally have not even begun to tap into the unfathomable amount of information and insight we can have if we connected with God. Especially when we face un-bearable circumstances and the unknown.

Speaking Of Unbearable Circumstances

If you ask me I'd have to say the most heart-felt passionate outcry of prayer in the whole Bible was done by Jesus himself in the gospels. This historical prayer encompasses all of the characteristics of God we just talked about. You know the story but have you ever stopped to contemplate the power of the words he spoke? Luke 22: 41 reads

> *He withdrew about a stones throw beyond them, knelt down and prayed. "Father if you are willing to take this cup from me. Yet not my will but yours be done." An angel from heaven appeared to Him and strengthened Him and being in anguish he prayed more earnestly and his sweat was like drops of blood falling to the ground.*

Have you ever had a prayer time like that before? Have you ever called out to God in such agony that it actually drains you physically and you sweat like drops of blood? Odds are probably not but it doesn't make our deepest prayer experiences anything less. It just challenges us to pray even harder. Cry out to God. Don't be ashamed tell Him how you feel and recognize who he is, what he can do and that He's there. Jesus did. What better example to follow.

Treading Water

Let me take you on a quick flashback for a minute. In my younger years I spent a lot of time at the YMCA. I took every swim class available on the roster and the swim team too. In one of our most difficult classes we trained how to tread water for extended amounts of time. Each week the instructor would add on another three to five minutes and before we knew it we had at gotten up to 30-45 minutes keeping our heads up in the middle of the deep end of the pool. Some shifts we would only be allowed to use our hands, others we would change to just our feet. Some weeks I remember we used just our feet while holding milk jugs half full of water above our heads. Through this exercise we strengthened our leg muscles and became better swimmers. I know it sounds like I was involved in some twisted Nazi training camp but I'm telling you the truth as I have my badges and awards to prove it! It was quite an accomplishment then. (Now days I would just put my highly trained gut up to the surface and let it keep me afloat).

I also remember as a teen when someone dared me to swim across a lake. Now let me explain this lake. Even though located in the Great Lake state of Michigan, it was not the size you probably pictured when I first said the word lake (like the one that separates Grand Haven, MI from Chicago.) It was a residential lake. Approximately the size of three maybe four blocks in your neighborhood. Yes that's still rather large but it's not the English Channel. I jumped in with all my ambition, energy and ability and swam as well as I could. Half way there and still no problem. Three quarters there now and feeling good. I finally made it and then remembered, ok now I have to go back. So I took a breath and started on my journey back across. By now I started to have a sinking feeling in my chest. (no pun intended). One-third of the way there and I had finally reached my max. My heart was pounding, my head spinning and I started panting like a dog.

This was a residential lake as I mentioned so there were many others people out on the lake. Most of them doing what you normally do on a lake. Water skiing, hanging on the boat soaking up the sun, etc. As for me I was just trying to win a bet. Then it happened and I finally lost all charisma. I reached my peak of energy and was done. I started to panic thinking my short life was over and looking frantically for assistance. Suddenly a boat

19

with a couple on board coasted up next to me. "Need a ride there champ?" he said with a hint of sarcasm in his voice. Without a word and embarrassed, I reached out and he pulled me in. We made it back to the other side in a matter of minutes and by the time we reached it I finally caught my breath and paid my dues.

S.O.S. : Save Our Souls

It doesn't matter if you grew up in the church and attended every worship service and event on the calendar. It doesn't matter how many Christian conferences you went to or Christian friends you have. You can listen to Christian music everyday and read every Christian book ever written. You can go to a Christian college and be trained on Church philosophy and theology day in and day out for the rest of your life. You can even have all the degrees and awards to prove it. No matter how much you surround yourself with a "Christian Life". I can still guarantee that pain, change, struggle and heartache are still going to come your way. There's no way to dodge it. Sometimes it may even seem more un-bearable than you can handle.

Life is like that. Always dishing up some new problem or catastrophe. We dare ourselves to swim past them and try pressing on towards the shore. You swim to the best of your ability thinking you might just be able to make it on your own as the waves toss you off course. You begin to feel your chest tighten up and your breath become very short. You then resort to paddling as long as you can while looking around desperately for any sign of land. Your heart begins to pound and then you stop. The only thing left is to tread water and begin to yell for help. You kick with your hands and your feet to keep your head afloat. You cry out as loud as you can. "Help me! Someone Help me!" "Is anyone out there?!" Just when all hope seems lost a small boat floats up beside you and you hear someone say "Need a ride there, friend?" You reach up and look at your rescuer. It's Jesus. Call out to God in your time of need. Worship Him. Those who call on the name of the Lord will be rescued and delivered from the depths of despair.

WHERE IN THE
WORLD ARE YOU?

"I cried out to God for help. I cried out to God to hear me. When I was in distress I sought the Lord at night I stretched out untiring hands and my soul refused to be comforted. I remembered you O God and I groaned. I mused and my sprit grew faint. You kept my eyes from closing I was too troubled too speak."

Psalm 77:1-4

A few days ago I was hanging at home relaxing when I noticed that my wife was extremely late coming home. I then began to impatiently wait and after about an hour I began to wonder. Where could she be? Is everything ok? I knew she had made an appointment for earlier that afternoon to visit with the teacher at my son's school so instead of calling and interrupting something I just sent her a text on my cell phone "Where are you?" In less than 30 seconds or so my phone beeped and she had replied. "Stopped at store be home soon." Great news to hear. A week ago I wrote my friend in L. A. an email. We keep in touch like that and I go out and visit him whenever I can. He returned my email the next day. It's always great to hear from an old friend. That's how the communication works. Message sent, message received, response is made, interaction takes place and the process is complete. However about 3 months ago I prayed a prayer to God. "God I need some answers only I know you can provide please let me know soon. This is my only request." I said Amen. No answer. I waited a week. No answer. I wanted a month no answer. Three months later....nothing.

Now if God had email, a cell phone or even text messaging I am sure I would keep trying to get in touch with him every way possible until I got some kind of response. That's how the process works remember. But instead the only way to get a hold of God is by what we know as prayer. It's pretty convenient I must say but it doesn't always make a lot of sense or seem to always trigger a response. Not in the time frame that I'm expecting it anyway. Often I feel like the obsessive boyfriend or girlfriend who can't let go of a relationship. "Hey why don't you ever return my calls? All I want to do is talk. Are you there? Pick up the phone! Please answer me! "Bad example I know but you get the point.

Where are you God? There is no doubt that this question is one we've all asked a time or two before. You pray and pray and wait and wait and yet there is never an answer or result to follow. What is the point? What is going on? Are you listening? Do you care? David in this Psalm expresses the same feelings as He is searching for God and not getting a reply. Check out some of the pretty defensive questions he asks later in this same chapter.

Will the Lord reject forever? Will He never show his favor again? Has His unfailing love vanished forever? Has God forgotten to be merciful? Has He in anger withheld his compassion?

Is anybody there?

I'd have to say it's obvious that David is really ticked off here. Why hasn't God replied? God I call out to you. I need help. I'm searching for you. I'm reaching for you. I'm desperate for you. Where are you? I'm thinking about you and my soul is weak. Where do you look for God anyway? Where do you find the all-powerful creator of the universe? Why doesn't He always answer when we call? He surely got my message. Is He too busy? David in this chapter begins to reminisce of everything God has done, all the times he as answered prayer and the promises He held to and realizes God has always been around so why give up on Him now.

There is a history of God in the world around us. God is present everywhere you go. Go is in the same place he was in when the sun, moon and stars were made. The same place he was when you were born and the same God he was when he offered up the perfect sacrifice to cover our sin. As a matter of fact He's in the same state, same town and same room as you. Why isn't He answering? I don't really know. It's not important that we know. Just that we learn to trust that He will. Sometime. Maybe now. Maybe later. Maybe not at all. (that is an answer in itself don't you think?) I think when we ask God "Why don't you answer me?" I think He's saying "Why don't you listen?" Have you ever listened for an answer? I have been doing that. I often forget though. Communication is a two way street remember. Sender-receiver, message sent-response given.

I've had times when I've tried to reach somebody and gotten mad that they never got back with me. Then I remember to check my voice mail and find they have contacted me I just totally missed the return call. Sometimes I think we aren't paying attention to God's answers. I can just picture seeing that flashing light on my phone. One new voicemail.

"Hey I've been trying to get a hold of you all week but I guess you've been to busy. I hear what you're going through and have been pulling you through all along as I always have. I will be here for you. I am listening I have plans for you so don't lose hope. I love You. I hope to hear from you again soon." The dial tone follows. Instantly my heart feels lighter again and I sigh in relief. God does respond we just to be open to hear what He has to say.

DEEPER

"Now if God had email, a cell phone or even text messaging I am sure I would keep trying to get in touch with him every way possible until I got some kind of response. That's how the process works remember. But instead the only way to get a hold of God is by what we know as prayer."

1. Have you ever wondered why God often seems to take a long time to reply?

2. Have you ever gotten a response from God quickly?

3. How did you feel when you finally got your answer?

DEFINITELY WORTH THE WAIT

*"I waited patiently for the Lord. He turned to me
and heard my cry. He lifted me out of the slimy pit,
out of the mud and mire; he set my feet on a rock
and gave me a firm place to stand. He put a new
song in my mouth a hymn of praise to our God."*

Psalm 40:1-3

Seven hours later I was still sitting there in the same spot. I
had gashed open the bottom of my foot and of all days, of course,
on my birthday. There I was sitting in the ER with nothing to do
and waiting for my turn to walk through that door and finally see
the Dr. face to face. Sound familiar? I know you would agree that
waiting is something that no one likes to do. Just the thought of
having to wait in itself is painful. Emergency Rooms seem to be
one of the worst places to wait. Dozens of strangers bleeding,
crying, looking extremely pale, shaking and in a blank stare. From
the ER to the customer service line at Wal-Mart, the layover for
your next flight, the line at the Motor Vehicle Department, or the
Post Office, nothing seems to be more miserable than waiting. It
isn't a favorite hobby in a world of instant and convenient.

David in the first few words of this scripture brings up these
horrible words we don't like to here. "Wait" and "patiently" On
top of that he was "waiting patiently" on God. Remember now
to God a day is like a thousand years. Talk about a long line.

25

There is no way around it though. Waiting is a part of the deal. We wait to find the answers to our questions, to find that new career we have been waiting for, to heal after an operation, to know what God wants from our lives and to see what life has in store for us next. It's not easy and it's not convenient. Through the trial David was going through he found that not just waiting but waiting patiently was the key to finding complete peace. To him it seems to be worth every second of the wait. "He heard my cry", he "lifted me from the slimy pit", he "set my feet on solid ground" and put a "new song in my mouth."

A lot of the time our conversations with God seem like routine and very one-sided. There is no answer and you feel like you just talked to yourself for no apparent reason. I'll be the first to say and admit I've prayed many prayers and for weeks and months without ever hearing an answer. It doesn't mean though it isn't being heard. We turn to God for help in time of need and for answers to the questions. In those situations there is normally nothing else we as humans can do. We find ourselves shouting out to God and wait to see what the answer is. We wait for the response. There is a reason why the word patiently is in this verse. That's what David discovered. He had to be patient and wait on God. For only God knows the perfect moment for the perfect answer for the situation you are overwhelmed by.

All we *can do* is wait patiently. All God *wants us to do* is wait patiently. All we *have to do* is wait patiently and then He turns his ear to our cry, He listens, He helps, He gives us hope, He gives us reason and on top of all that gives a reason to praise. Ok let's review. What do we have to do? We patiently wait. What does God do in return? He listens, lifts us up, gives us hope and puts a new song in our hearts. What a deal!! Doesn't that make waiting sound so much easier? You do the math.

We will wait in the ER for hours in pain because we know when our turn comes we will find the treatment we need to be cured. We sit in the room at the M.V. D. until our magic number is called because we know we will get our license renewed again.

We wait in line at Taco Bell behind 10 cars so we can get our hands on that food we've been craving for. We wait in the massive crowd of people at the airport for our delayed flight because we know we will at some time reach our final destination and return home again. Waiting on God seems so much harder since it sometimes seems to never end.

The reality though is that the rewards and promise of waiting on God patiently no matter what the case is much greater and long term. Yes the wait would seem so much easier and convenient if we could only see what's at the other end. David however gives us a glimpse of what is on the other end in this very verse. "I waited patiently for the Lord" and in return "He lifted me out of the slimy pit, out of the mud and mire, he set my feet on a rock and gave me a firm place to stand. He put a new song in my mouth a hymn of praise to our God."

What I can learn personally from this is that if I know God has some kind of answer for me and will hear my cry, give me hope and put the passion back into life then there is no doubt you will find me waiting patiently on the other end anytime. It's easier said than done. But what do you have to lose. You're not going anywhere. Take a seat.

Deeper

> *"All we can do is wait patiently. All God wants us to do is wait patiently. All we have to do is wait patiently and then He turns his ear to our cry, He listens, He helps, He gives us hope, He gives us reason and on top of all that gives a reason to praise"*

1. What is the longest you have ever waited on God?

2. What did you learn in the waiting process?

3. Did you continue worshipping Him while waiting?

A CASE OF THE BROKENHEARTED

"The righteous cry out and the Lord hears them. He delivers them from all their troubles. The Lord is close to the brokenhearted and saves those who are crushed in spirit. A righteous man may have many troubles but the Lord delivers him from them all. He protects all his bones, not one of them will be broken."

Psalms 34:17-20

It's probably safe to say that sometime in your life at one time or another you have experienced a break up. You may have been dumped by a high school sweet heart, ditched by a favorite somebody or even left by a spouse. As you know it's painful. We live in a world that is broken. Promises are broken, dreams are broken relationships are broken but there is nothing as painful as being heartbroken.

We all know a heart can't be literally broken. It just feels that way when love is ripped away and you are left feeling crushed, worthless or lonely. Let me ask you to think with me about the phrase heart broken. A short English class if you don't mind. First is the word heart. Referring to what is being talked about here. It is the subject. Broken is the word to follow. Referring to what happened to the heart. Now let's go to the next level. If you own a pet this might be easier to understand. Take for example the phrase House-broken. This of course does not mean your house has been broken. The phrase house broken is a way of saying that you have trained your pet to either use his or her litter-box or go outside when he or she feels the need to relieve their bladder. (Now you can see why they keep it to just the phrase housebroken. Easier to say, better word picture.) Brokenhearted on the other hand means something totally different then heart broken. The way it is used here means "to be totally sold out to God." It's being broken completely of ourselves and taking on the nature of God. Broken of what used to drive us and totally driven by God and his will.

Being brokenhearted is not easy in any way but what is comforting when referring to this verse is to know that God is close to those who are brokenhearted. People who are brokenhearted often feel that God is far away from them when really He is closer than ever. They cry out to God in their brokenness and he hears their cry. It also says he delivers them from their troubles and saves those crushed in spirit. Being broken hearted does mean God will be present it also means though that you will be full of questions and no answers at first as you wait to see what God is going to pull out of the hat for you and your life now that you are totally His. Dr. Bob Laurent a professor at Bethel College in Mishawaka, Indiana says it in a unique way. He said," He doesn't always give you all the answers. He gives us himself." Even Jesus himself had questions and was broken hearted as he hung on the cross and shouted. "My God, my God, why do you forsake me?"

God can't bear to be separated from his children who are hurting so he draws near to them. He has a passion for those who are brokenhearted and for those who are truly searching for Him. I see this process happen with my kids a lot. My youngest boy got the flu bug and the oldest started getting jealous of all the attention and benefits the other was getting. "Why does he get the new Spiderman band-aids? Why does he get a Popsicle?

How come he gets to stay up late and has been right with you all day long?"

"Because he's the one that is sick and we are trying to care for him," I'd answer. I t makes sense to the parent but not the child who might feel like he's getting the shaft. The sick are the ones who need the constant intense care. So there I am on the couch snuggling with the Mr. sick. In the same way broken people need God's care. God is close to them in their brokenness.

Shadrach, Mesach and Abendego. Great examples of names you will never find in a baby book. Even better, they are great illustrations of men who were totally brokenhearted and sold out to God. Even to the point of death by burning. "If they don't worship me they will be tossed into the furnace," was the king's decree. All three of them in their obedience to their God didn't worship the king. All three of them were tossed into the fire. Three went in. Four people were counted in the fire. God is close to the brokenhearted.

You might be lost or confused and spend your time praying and crying out to him in need. If you are totally relying on God and are sold out to Him in your time of need you are experiencing broken-heartedness and it's a promise that God himself is right there next to you.

Deeper

"Brokenhearted on the other hand means something totally different then heart broken. The way it is used here means "to be totally sold out to God." It's being broken completely of ourselves and taking on the nature of God. Broken of what used to drive us and totally driven by God and his will."

1. Describe a few things that come to your mind when you hear the word "broken-hearted".

2. Has any problem in your life that you have encountered ever left you broken- hearted?

3. What one thing may be keeping you from being totally sold out to God?

IS THIS THING ON?

O Lord the God who saves me, day and night
I cry out before you. May my prayer come
before You. Turn your ear to my cry.

Psalm 88:1-2

"What was that?" My body felt like a giant slug but my brain had just gone on instant alert. I heard a noise in the house and it was 3 or so in the middle of the night. I heard it again. This time I cracked one eye open to try to be a little more alert and listened a little harder. It didn't work. Fifteen minutes later I was awoken again by this awkward little noise and then decided maybe I should actually sit up and listen more intently. (Still too lazy to actually remove myself from the bed) There it was a short small whining kind of sound. Reluctantly I stepped onto the floor and wobbled out the door and into the hallway. The sound happened again. I it was coming from my youngest son's room. "What's up buddy, you ok?" I asked. The sound I had been hearing was none other than a quiet cry for dad as he was laying there waiting for me to come in. "Daddy I had a bad dream, can you stay in here until I fall back asleep?" Of course I stayed and in seconds he was out cold and I too drifted back into my coma.

Anyone who is a parent or watches over children knows that they depend on their parents to give them support and be there in time of need. Children know that if they cry or call out for us we will be there to assist and provide. You could not find a better firsthand example of the same kind of relationship with God and his creations. David in Psalm 88, is the child calling out to God to connect with Him in the middle of his heartache and looking for some comfort. Hoping that someone would be able to hear him and bring resolve. Prayer, as simple as it seems is more complex, powerful and effective than we realize. That is something David has come to learn and he again in Psalm 88 has found himself looking to God to fill the need.

In this prayer three major things really jump out at me that I have noticed personally are good to keep in mind when facing difficulty. First of all in the very beginning words of his plea you can find him recognizing that God will save Him. "O Lord the God who saves me," He's evidently experienced this pain before as again he comes before God with his personal request looking to be rescued. David knew God could help and would if he cried out in prayer. Second, he continues on and as it says he cries out day and night nonstop. That's some serious prayer going on. Not many of us do that. Praying day and night. That's when you can tell that the request and the need is heavy on your heart. Finding yourself in the "prayer mode" throughout the day every day shows you are seeking God's will intently and you are passionate about it.

He worshipped God, he called on God and he made his request known to God. That's the third part. He called on God. He simply just asks for his request to be presented and for God to hear his cry. Notice he didn't say "Answer my request or else! Or "why don't you listen to me?" No belligerence or arrogance. Just a simple plea. He humbly asked God to hear his cry and to listen to his request.

Many times when I get frustrated about praying I think of the cell phone commercial everyone is familiar with. The slogan that rings so true, "Can you hear me now?" I can think of the numerous amounts of times I've been on the phone in the middle of an important conversation and all of the sudden I get cut off. Or better yet when you make a call and the person on the other end can't hear you although you hear them perfectly.

Them: "Hello"

Me: "Hey how are you?"

Them: "Hello?!"

Me: HEY I'M HERE! I said How are you?"

Them: "I can't hear you, is anyone there?"

Me: HEELLOO! You've got to be kidding me! I hear you fine.

Them: "Sorry I can't hear anything call again later."

You know how it goes. Sometimes just being heard is all that really counts. I just want to be heard that's all. Am I talking to myself? Is anyone listening? You leave the message. Never get a reply. Send the email, never get a return. Is anyone out there? Testing 1, 2, 3 is this thing on? Somebody please listen. *"Turn your ear to my cry"* All he wanted is just to be heard. "May my prayer come before you" He had spoken his request and now awaited a response. Communication with God is a guaranteed two way street although it doesn't seem like it at all. We may think we are not being heard when the conversation is really going something like this..

Us: Hello. I cry out to you and hope you can hear me.

God: I can hear you. Can you hear me?

Us: Listen to my prayer O God. Please listen to my cry

God: I hear you and will answer your requests

Us: Hello God can you hear me? I cry out to you day and night.

God: I've been listening

Us: Please hear me. I will continue to call on you again

God: I'll be waiting

Deeper

"David in Psalm 88, is the child calling out to God to connect with Him in the middle of his heartache and looking for some comfort. Hoping that someone would be able to hear him and bring resolve. Prayer, as simple as it seems is more complex, powerful and effective than we realize. That is something David has come to learn and he again in Psalm 88 has found himself looking to God to fill the need."

1. Ever feel like you not being heard?

2. Have you ever called out to God in a time of desperation?

3. Do you believe God hears our prayers even if He doesn't answer? How do you explain that?

FEARLESS

God is our refuge and strength, an ever present help in trouble. Therefore we will not fear though the earth gives way and the mountains fall into the heart of the sea.

Psalm 46:1-2

I feel like it's the end of the world. My life is caving in and I just can't take it anymore. If those words have ever come out of your mouth or floated around in your head then this verse is for you. Notice David again re-iterates the omnipresent factor in this Psalm firsthand as He declares God is our "ever present" help in trouble. David himself knew what it meant to have your world cave in and to feel like life as you know it is over. From physical attacks on his flock by a bear and lion, to the challenge of facing the Philistine giant, to being attacked by the king himself and then his fall into the trap of temptation. When going through so many different personal struggles its good to have a "refuge" or friend to lean on and hold you accountable. Someone to give you strength through whatever comes your way. David had that and even though he didn't always rely on it, the friend was always there. I recently ran across an old seven volume commentary by Charles H. Spurgeon published in 1885. These words are so profound that I wanted to share them with you. Listen to his explanation of this first verse.

37

God is our refuge and strength, Not our armies, or our fortresses. Israel's boast is in Jehovah, the only living and true God. Others vaunt their impregnable castles, placed on inaccessible rocks, and secured with gates of iron, but God is a far better refuge from distress than all these: and when the time comes to carry the war into the enemy's territories, the Lord stands his people in better stead than all the valor of legions or the boasted strength of chariot and horse. Soldiers of the cross, remember this, and count yourselves safe, and make yourselves strong in God. Forget not the personal possessive word our; make sure each one of your portion in God, that you may say, "He is my refuge and strength." Neither forget the fact that God is our refuge just now, in the immediate present, as truly as when David penned the word. God alone is our all in all. All other refuges are refuges of lies; all other strength is weakness, for power belongeth unto God: but as God is all sufficient, our defense and might are equal to all emergencies.

A very present help in trouble, or in distress he has so been found, he has been tried and proved by his people. He never withdraws himself from his afflicted. He is their help, truly, effectually, constantly; he is present or near them, close at their side and ready for their succour, and this is emphasized by the word very in our version, he is more present than friend or relative can be, yea, more nearly present than even the trouble itself. To all this comfortable truth is added the consideration that his assistance comes at the needed time. He is not as the swallows that leave us in the winter; he is a friend in need and a friend indeed.

I love those words "more nearly present than even the trouble itself." Think about that. Though overwhelmed by problems surrounding you, God is closer. He's right up in your business. Smack dab in the front of any crisis or heartache that comes your way. Even though David faced every sort of challenge and frustration and was burdened by it He still found himself overwhelmed by the power of God. That is what so often kept him on his toes and gave him the strength to keep coming back for more when facing trials. The Psalms are full of his stories in lyrical fashion pouring out every emotion in anger and praise as He proclaimed a God who protects and provides. "God is our refuge and strength". Sure he didn't always choose the God route when facing everything but whether he did or not time and time again God proved himself to be around to depend on, fall back on and use in a time of retreat.

We've got nothing to worry about. We should be extremely optimistic. With God on our side, fear itself is completely irrational. We are in a win win situation. The earth can give way and mountains crash. All change can happen in a moments notice and all faith can be challenged but God still remains. Not only is God's love preserved from the beginning of time to eternity but so is his ability to preserve us from any harm along the way. With God our ever-present help in trouble what ever could destroy us? Just the thought of that can bring satisfaction through any dilemma that comes your way.

Deeper

> *"He is their help, truly, effectually, constantly; he is present or near them, close at their side and ready for their succour, and this is emphasized by the word very in our version, he is more present than friend or relative can be, yea, more nearly present than even the trouble itself.'*

1. Have you ever felt God's presence in a time of trouble or fear?

2. What comes to mind when you hear the words, "God is our refuge"?

3. What in the documentary by Charles Spurgeon stands out to you the most?

CHAPTER 3:

SINK OR SWIM OR PADDLE LIKE CRAZY

Singer, Songwriter, worship leader and author Matt Redman once wrote these words. *"The heart of God loves a persevering worshipper who though overwhelmed by many troubles is overwhelmed even more by the beauty of God."* This simple quote has made an enormous impact on my life as a worshipper and as a worship leader. So simple, so true and so much the focus of what this whole book is about. The word overwhelmed mentioned here is one we all can relate to and define. You might be even feeling a bit overwhelmed right now. But have you ever stopped to ponder the concept of being overwhelmed by the beauty of God?

Several years ago we took a week vacation in California. I love visiting California because it's such a beautiful place. Especially along the coast. We spent a day or two just driving along Route One there, which follows the cliff where the mountains meet the sea. I had never been there so when I came around the corner and saw it, it stole my breath away. We drove quite a ways down astonished at the wonder of creation and then just stopped. We got out of the car, stepped up to the edge and just stood in disbelief. No words can ultimately describe your feelings when you sense God's beauty through the wonder of his creation. If you live in California you might be saying," sure it's just a large body of water and some hills" but you have to admit it does leave you in awe. Creation speaks volumes of Gods beauty and so does life itself. We are blessed with so much and even more as Christians. Even when struggles come our way if you look beyond the pain and confusion you can find God's beauty not only around us but in the dilemma we are facing. He has the ability to use even our greatest pain for something bigger and better. When you can see it that way it makes even the biggest catastrophe, even the feeling of drowning in life itself, a sea of spiritual opportunities.

Perseverance Power

The other word Redman mentions here is "persevering". Ironically this is not a word many can relate to. Will power, determination, boldness, strength. Not at all at first the words or thoughts that go through your mind when in crisis mode. It's something you learn once you have been through the crisis and have made it to the other side. You have seen the whole picture. Then you can persevere knowing there is a "higher perspective" and plan for life. Worshipping God through the trials is what leads to the power to see that higher perspective. I've heard it said before that "Worship possesses the power to make the problems you face seem small while magnifying other things." It "possesses a supernatural ability to correct our spiritual vision problems and bring everything into divine focus." That's where the power of perseverance comes in. It's not a trait easily learned but once it is learned it makes everything so much easier. God has a plan for all and is in control of everything. Good and bad. It doesn't make sense from our viewpoint why God would let bad things happen in any shape or form. It's not his nature. I don't understand. But I know God in all His glory can take a bad situation and change it around to have a good outcome. So if He can use a bad experience to make a good change in our hearts and lives then I say bring it on! Through his love He makes all things new and good. God's love does not fail! Speaking of failure. I often find myself overwhelmed that God would even take the time to pull me through any personal mess I find myself in knowing that I might end up there again but we are His creations. He strives to make us better and stronger through all any crisis that comes our way. Whether crisis that we ourselves created in our own human nature or even initiated naturally by life itself. Caring for His children is what matters most to God. It's the foundation of His love. It's His passion.

What's Your Motive?

What is your motive? What is your passion? Often this word is tied in with many negative connotations. Sex, lust, desire greed, idolatry. On the flip side of the coin the word passion means so much more as it is the core of what drives us and makes us tick. Just as Christ is passionate in all He has done, is doing and will do He has created us to be passionate too. When you hear the word passion what's the first thing that you think of? When I think of the word passion here are some of the words that come to mind: Motivation, feeling alive, dynamic, vitality, full, inspiration, on fire, intensity, adventure, drive, satisfaction, reason. All of these words are great to help define what passion is but hard to relate to if you have altogether lost it. It's incredible that with the craziness of schedules, business and stress that we even have an ounce of passion left in us at all. There is hardly any time allowed for God in your daily schedule after planning everything else first. You can really see what you worship the most by looking at your planner. Every hour of the day is taken up with meetings, job, school, appointments, responsibilities, kids, chores and so much more. So many events crammed and packed into a daily schedule but no God. We have lost focus of why we are here on this planet. We have lost our one true passion in life as so many other priorities take precedent in our agendas in place of priority number one.

My Passion

Outside of my passion to serve God, my family and build strong relationships my next greatest passion is music. I love music. If I'm not listening to it I'm playing it. If I'm not playing it I'm writing it and playing on my guitar or keyboard. It's my favorite pastime, it's my hobby, it's my career, and it's my life. I have hundreds of CDs I play dozens of songs on my MP3 player almost everyday. I have subscriptions to music magazines, collect books on musical topics and frequently attend concerts of all kinds. I find satisfaction in writing music. I find enjoyment in listening to it. Most of all though, I love to use it as a tool to minister to people and to worship God. That is the ultimate satisfaction and enjoyment of music for me. That is my passion. I have always been involved in music in one way or another, my whole life and have discovered over the years how God gave me the gift of music and creativity. Using this gift to serve in return completes the cycle and brings full-fillment in every way. When I'm not using that gift I know I'm missing out and I desire to again use it however I can. It's one of the few things that drives me and gives me purpose in life.

Why do I bring up passion and purpose in this chapter? Because our passion is what drives us and motivates us. The question to think about here is what motivates you? In Rick Warren's best seller "The Purpose Driven Life" he lists some other unique things people are driven by. If you have read through this book before you will remember these. They include guilt, resentment and anger, fear, materialism and the need for approval. These are some of the things that drive people through life in general. Whether positive or negative these things help to understand overall what people use to give them ambition. Let's go even deeper. What is it that can drive you to persevere through the challenges of life? Is it what you were created for or is it your own personal agenda? I guarantee that if you are truly passionate about God's purpose for your life you will find hope beyond measure and trust in all circumstances. The main passion we are not only required but naturally wired to pursue is to the desire to know our creator, grow closer with him daily and love and serve him more. That is overall the meaning of every one of our lives. To know God, grow in God, love and serve God. If that isn't part of our daily routine there is no doubt you will find yourself drowning and sinking fast.

Think of it this way. What in the world really deserves all my time, all my attention and worship? Better yet what in the world is worth worshipping or being totally passionate about? Don't think too hard. When it comes to difficulties in your life the bottom line is this. Are you going to make the best of it or let it get the best of you? He goes on to state that Knowing your purpose helps to give meaning, simplify life, help you find a focus and to find motivation. It's obvious that we are created with purpose and when we discover it, it helps us to have a new clearer perspective through the good and the bad

The Passion to Persevere

When I think of passion and perseverance I can't help but picturing a great example we all know as the author of most of the New Testament. I would love to be able to spend a day with this guy and watch him in action. From mass murderer to missionary. He had suddenly found his passion in life and not only changed his lifestyle but even his name. Paul was a man who was on fire for God and had a desire to use every second of every day to serve God no matter what came his way. As you know the problems did come his way. He was like a magnet for chaos and trouble. It couldn't stay away from him. Paul's journey and adventures puts Indiana Jones movies to shame. His character put the power in perseverance. His love for God trumped all heartache that came his way. Shipwrecked, beaten, ridiculed, abandoned by friends, bitten by a snake, imprisoned numerous times, put on trial, opposed by powerful leaders just to name a few. The amazing part of it all is that never did his passion to persevere fade away.

As a matter of fact it seemed in those moments of turmoil for Paul, the flame of his passion burned even brighter. Many books of the New Testament were written while he was in chains in jail! Think about that. Worshipping God through writing, praying and singing while at rock bottom. Now that's real passion. That's being totally overwhelmed by God's beauty and love.

> *"Love is as strong as death, its jealousy unyielding as the grave, It burns like blazing fire. Many waters cannot quench love, rivers cannot wash it away." Song of Songs 8:6-7*

The Count of Monte Cristo

I am a huge Star wars fan and always have been. I've been excited about each movie that ever came out in that series since it first started back in 1979. I only have had a handful of other movies that are my all time favorites and one of those is *The Count of Monte Cristo*. If you have not seen this film you have to go get it. Put this book down, drive to your local video store, order it online or whatever. Just go watch it. If you don't I am about to ruin the whole thing for you as I tell you about some of my favorite parts. If you chose to read on and you haven't seen the movie then well, at least you will be familiar with this part and you can look forward to seeing it firsthand. Then again you can always stop reading now. Or now. Or… I'd say just skip over it but then you'd miss the whole point of this chapter. Ok you are still reading. Well at least I warned you.   Here we go.

In this epic movie the main character, Edmond Dantes played by Jim Cavizel, is framed by the government for being involved in an act of treason. He is reluctantly sent to an island prison called the Chateau D'if where he was sentenced to remain in a cell for his lifetime as their way to cover up this innocent man from informing anyone of the truth. A political scandal. Seven years into his captivity he still remained in desperation trying to find reason to live. In his cell he found engraved on the wall the

words " God will give me justice" and daily with a rock he would
sketch into these words emphasizing each letter making it deeper
as he went and metaphorically etching these words into his mind
as a way to cope and make it by. "God will give me justice. A few
years later he gave up. He lost his vision and his passion to go on
and tried to hang himself. After much contemplation he began to
be disenchanted by God giving justice since God had not in any
way helped through these painful years and he in return decided
that the only revenge he would ever have would have to be taken
into his own hands and he was filled with anger.

Meanwhile in a cell or two over another inmate who had
been in for much longer had spent five years of his time digging a
tunnel to break out only to find he had dug in the wrong direction
and popped up in the floor of Dantes room. After meeting and
sharing how they had spent the past several years of their lives.
The older man took him back to his cell through the tunnel in
the floor. This is where the conversation first started that really
hit home. The older man had talked about God and how he had
helped him through to which Edmond replied.

"There is no talk of God here priest"

"What about the inscription?" the priest asked (referring to
the phrase, "God will give me justice"

"It is faded just as God from my heart"

"And what has replaced it?"

"Revenge!"

Driven by the opportunity to get revenge he helped the priest
dig the tunnel in the right direction. Driven by passion itself
the priest continued in his journey to freedom. Just a few inches
of dirt dug a week to reach a little under 4 meters a year they
continued on to the other side. As they reached the last few feet
the tunnel caved in and the priest suffered a severe puncture to
his chest. In his final words be began in a heartfelt conversation
with Edmond. Knowing he was driven by revenge alone he said
in his dying breath…

"Do not commit the crime to which you now serve the sentence. God said vengeance is mine"

"I don't believe in God" he responded.

And with death in his eyes he said to him "Edmond, he believes in *you*"

Have you lost your passion and vision? Do you think God has given up? Amazingly when we feel we are furthest from Him, He is closer then ever. God remains passionate about us even when we lose all passion in Him.

The Break Up

I remember my first break up. Do you remember when you were first dumped? Those things are hard to forget and funny to think back on later. I was standing there on the sidewalk in my hometown when I heard those gut-wrenching words. "It's over. I've found somebody else and am moving on. "At that moment I remember being struck dumb with nothing to say. I wasn't sure what just happened but I was pretty sure it wasn't good. My heart sank. The words burnt like fire and my whole world began to shatter. Sure it was one of those high school dating experiences but the world seems so much smaller when you're a teen and a break up seems to somehow put an end to that small world. My heart was like a giant lump of playdough, each word like another punch to smash it just a little more flatter.

"It's over."

"Ouch"

"I've found someone else"

"Someone stop the pain!"

"I'm moving on"

"Ah get off your killing me! "

I remember the following days and weeks feeling like years passing by. Love was gone and life was boring. You begin to find yourself with little or no excitement and all normal daily routines have gone out the window.

It's not until you rediscover love again that it all comes back.

When your life becomes a scheduled routine centered on anything and everything but God himself, in a sense you have "broken up" with him. It's as if you are saying "There are other important things to focus on now God. There is someone else." You're passion is lost, your love for Him has begun to dissipate and you are living for yourself. It's no wonder we lose all hope and perseverance if God is removed. It's in those times we need to turn back to God and pour out our hearts. I love you God. I want to go deeper into your love. Help me to be more passionate and use my life only for you. I need you. I'm desperate for you.

Life's heartaches, pain and difficulties can overwhelm but God is always much bigger. Finding God in those heartaches, pains and difficulties only bring love back into the picture and passion back into your life. As a matter of fact maybe that's the whole problem. You have lost your drive, your will to survive, your ambition to use your life for something greater, and your desire to move on past the present difficulties. You've been so bogged down by your own life that you totally forgot to include God in any of it. You dumped God only to realize that He is the one and only true love of your life. You have been trying to live life for yourself only to find that you are now trying to save yourself. Caught up in the fear of drowning you have totally missed your whole passion for living.

The Bottom Line

There you are surrounded by the endless waves and ocean surface. You have been swimming for days headed for the shore that is not visible for miles. You are panting desperately for the chance to be rescued. Your hope is beginning to dissolve. Faith in being helped in any possible way has disappeared and your strength and will power to hold on for even another minute is unbearable. You are at a crossroads in life and the decision to sink or swim, to press on no matter what comes your way or just give in is yours to make. Sink or swim. Dive deep into the passion of

God and again find your strength to go on or sink while losing all hope in yourself. Do you want to make the best of the situation of have the situation get the best of you?

Maybe you were on fire for God and got distracted along the way. Maybe you never included God as part of your daily schedule and life and now find yourself discovering how much you need him as you are lost at sea. It may even be that your lack of passion for God is what put you where you are right now in your life. You lost your focus, you lost your passion now you have found yourself in need of Him again. In Matthew you can find the amazing story of how Peter in this same situation lost his focus. After seeing Jesus walking on the water got out of the boat and started to walk on the water towards him. Matthew 14:30 says, "But when he saw the wind, he was afraid and beginning to sink cried out. "Lord, save me".

The problem here is when he lost sight of God. He saw the wind and was afraid. He was overwhelmed by the problem around him and not by the presence of God. In our own issues we lose sight of God and begin to sink and drown. Our passion is designed to not only give us incentive and a drive to do what we were created to do in the good times but also to pull us through in the bad. Passion is not the feeling we get when we had a great night sleep and feel like we are ready to take on the world. Instead passion is a fire that drives us to have that feeling to take on the world even if we only slept for 1hour all night long. Passion is not the feeling you get when life is great, when you are feeling on top of the world and loving life. It's the desire that motivates you to feel on top of the world and loving life even in the midst of death and despair. If your passion and focus in life is truly centered on Jesus when problems still come your way He will help you see beyond it all. If you persevere through the hardship keeping your passion alive and remain in an attitude of worship at all times you be able to see and know that there is a way out, an answer, hope and healing not to far away. Perseverance is hard to understand when you feel you are going to snap. Perseverance from a personal perspective is one of the most difficult things I've ever had to deal with. I don't always get it. I really don't like it at all. It doesn't seem normal. That's my human nature. I still get this gut feeling though that it's my best choice and will be worth it somehow. And I still hear a small voice constantly saying these simple yet helpful words. "Fix your eyes on Jesus."

GIVE IT UP

Trust in the Lord with all your heart, lean not on your own understanding. In all your ways acknowledge Him and He will make your paths straight

Proverbs 3: 5- 6

I remember several years ago when I was headed to the Sandusky, Ohio area for a concert with a group of friends. I'm not sure why but I got directions to the venue off an internet site that has let me down a couple times before. To make a long story short, it happened again. The map led us from a major highway, to a side street, to a long country road through a never ending cornfield and before I knew it I had led the group to a small dark village on what looked like a set of the Twilight Zone. What were people thinking when they programmed the directions to this place. I can just see a bunch of guys sitting around a table making up suggestions for these directions. "Hey I got an idea let's totally mess these roads up and see we can sucker into getting totally lost." (enter myself here) Maybe they throw darts at the map and connect dots. Whatever the case my guess is that their ultimate goal is not to provide legit directions but to find a cruel way to get a quick laugh. For us ironically, it was a memorable and extremely funny experience but we honestly had no idea where we were and I admit at first this little town gave me the creeps. (I won't mention the name of this direction based website but it does rhyme with … "not the best") It's true we have all gotten lost before but for me it seems to be a curse. I myself often try to call shotgun as much as I can and have some other lucky person drive so we can all get there preferably within the allotted time frame. The way I see it, it's to everyone's advantage in the long run. Who wants to take 2 days to just get on the other side of town anyway?

This verse reminds me a lot of looking for directions. Come on, you have to admit it. It's a verse that a lot of us have heard millions of times but have never truly taken to heart. When you're in a time of searching and trying to find God's direction in your life this verse really says it all and means so much more than we take it for. I think the key word in the first part of this verse is the word *all*. We often give a lot of ourselves to pursuing whatever it is we are doing but not 100%.

We are usually wrapped up in so much on a daily basis that it's hard to totally give all of yourself to anything. It's difficult to be sold out to one thing and not just spread thin amongst a dozen others. We work at our jobs but are thinking about all the things we'd rather be doing. We hang with our families and loved ones but often focus on everything but them. We go to church and sit there in our seat yet our hearts and minds are filled with distractions it can almost make you feel worn out. We are easily distracted and lost in our own world, on our own maps that are leading us in circles. We need some new directions. Directions that lead us to a place where we can find a final destination and feel we have arrived. Directions that are easy to follow and that we can trust.

In this verse it simply says "Trust in the Lord with ALL of your heart." Notice it doesn't say with 50% of your heart, or just a majority of it. It says all. It's knowing God is 100% totally trustworthy and being sold old to His directions. I wish there was some natural way as humans to let go of our own understanding and control and give it up to someone else. We try to make sense of everything and process the world around us through our limited viewpoint. Usually our thoughts and understanding of the world around us only leads us further away from the truth. The words *"With all your heart"* mean to passionately pursue after God and follow his path. The word *ALL* actually comes up again later in the verse. "In *all of your ways acknowledge Him"*. So we are to trust in the Lord with all our heart, Lean not on your own understanding and in all of our ways acknowledge him. Three major directions to better get to reach our final destination.

He will make your paths straight. This is for sure. No more wrong turns or bad directions. No more confusion, heartache or hurt about where you have ended up. Literally. Give it up. Give it ALL up. You are in the passenger seat and He will do the driving. Move over. Just trust Him. Have you ever seen anyone actually ask an airline pilot "um... excuse me but do you actually know where you're going?" Probably not. Trust God. You don't have to understand where He might be driving you to. Just know that he will get you to exactly where you need to go. Acknowledge that He actually might know how to get there and it might be easier than you thought.   He might even know a shortcut.   Believe me He doesn't need a backseat driver so my suggestion would be get in. Wait it out. See where the road leads and learn to trust that He will get you there.   It's better than getting lost.........
again.... and again..... and again.......

Deeper

In this verse it simply says "Trust in the Lord with ALL of your heart." Notice it doesn't say with 50% of your heart, or just a majority of it. It says all. It's knowing God is 100% totally trustworthy and being sold old to His directions.

1. Have you ever felt completely lost?

2. Do you have enough faith in God to trust where He might lead?

3. How does our daily worship show our trust in God?

SUFFERING = HOPE?
SAY WHAT?

"We also rejoice in our sufferings because we know that suffering produces perseverance, perseverance character and character hope."

Romans 5:3-4

There's that word again. The word that doesn't really fit. The word that doesn't make sense at first when related to suffering. It's the word rejoice. Rejoice in suffering. It's such a hard concept to fathom, yet the only key to real joy. Who would have ever thought that something as negative as suffering accompanied by something so uplifting as rejoicing could ever lead to something as positive as hope. The answer is no one but God.

Suffering is something we all can relate to. Hope on the other hand isn't. To be hopeful there has to be some kind of evidence or proof that the bad stuff will eventually fade away. True hope in God covers all the frustrations that come your way. Reaching out and grasping hold of that true hope in God that is the main challenge. This verse is a formula, if you will on how to find hope through the bad even when the problem may at first be so overwhelming that there seems to be no way out.

First comes the suffering. There is usually no real warning when this kind of stuff is going to pop up its ugly head. If they only had something similar to a meteorologist for these kinds of things. You know, like someone to inform us so we can be aware of what's coming our way and maybe even be prepared. Maybe a "Crisis-ologist" or something.

"Well today will be partly happy and then we will experience a few showers of depression and oh wait there seems to be a front of something coming in here. Looks like a major personal struggle or maybe just a bad hair day. Good news is that sometime soon, possibly early next week but maybe next month we will be back in to happy and clear skies. Until then keep your head up don't stop breathing. Back to you Dave."

We aren't always aware of when a tragedy, personal struggle or crisis might occur or even how long it might last but we can be sure according to this verse that through it we have the opportunity to learn all about perseverance.

Perseverance as anyone knows is not one of our favorite hobbies. So if the situation isn't already a struggle enough on top of that we are to develop a sense of perseverance which seems to be the icing on the cake. If it isn't already a pain we have to go against our natural instinct to give up and find a way to press on, to go against the wind, to face up to the junk. (Whether we like it or not.) Perseverance from there leads to character. Character is a good thing in this whole process. After all character defines who we are and if perseverance can improve or make your character more Christ-like or hopeful then in the long run it makes all the other worth it. That's our goal in life anyway isn't it? To try to be more like our maker even if it stings a little or hurts a lot?

Perseverance leads to character and character leads to hope. Hope is a good word. Hope is a great word. Hope is what keeps most of us going each day. Hope that we will get our daily tasks done. Hope that we will be successful at our careers. Hope that our kids will do well in school. Hope that we will continue to be blessed with health and prosperity. Without hope we have nothing. So to sum it all up Hope is developed by suffering.

Suffering leads to hope. Still sounds weird but believe me it is true.

You might recall a little green guy familiar to the big screen who once spoke words similar to this verse we are looking at. No I'm not talking about Kermit. I'm referring to a wise and very old hero we all know as Yoda. Yes another Star Wars example again. He's the perfect illustration to use here. Two different times in the Star Wars trilogies he quoted these words when judging the character of a young Padawan Jedi . Check it out. Better yet put on your best Yoda voice and read it out loud.

"Fear leads to anger, anger leads to hate, hate leads to suffering." Remember these words? This is nothing but truth and wisdom from a philosophical, wrinkly, totally fictitious space character who likes to talk in riddles. We fear the unknown. We fear what problems may come our way and we become angry with ourselves and with God. We ask out loud, "What are you doing to me God? I'm tired of this! "Our anger builds and leads to hate and bitterness. Hate leads to pain and suffering. We live in our suffering until we continue on with these great thoughts from Paul to the Romans. Words that bring a whole new twist to struggle and put a smile on your face.

Suffering leads to perseverance, perseverance leads to character, character leads to......... hope.

Deeper

> *"Suffering is something we all can relate to. Hope on the other hand isn't. To be hopeful there has to be some kind of evidence or proof that the bad stuff will eventually fade away. True hope in God covers all the frustrations that come your way. Reaching out and grasping hold of that true hope in God that is the main challenge."*

1. Have you ever found yourself worshipping God when absolutely everything seems to be going wrong?

2. Have you ever experienced the power of hope?

3. How can our worship to God lead to the hope we all need?

COMPLETELY COMPLETED

"Consider it pure joy my brothers whenever you face trials of many kinds because you know that the testing of your faith develops perseverance. Perseverance must finish its work so that you may be mature and complete not lacking in anything."

James 1:2-4

I remember when I graduated from high school. Now that was pure excitement. Or when my sons were born. I was overflowing with Joy. Or riding the Top Thrill Dragster at Cedar Point, or going on that long awaited family vacation to Florida, or when I found $100 in one of my old school books. Nothing but sheer ultimate happiness. But never in my life have I ever found any happiness when facing crisis. That's just not normal. What in the world was he thinking when he wrote this? What could possibly be exciting about going through something difficult? Joy and "trials of life" are on the opposite ends of the spectrum.

There's a key word here and the first time I read it I missed it totally. The key word here is, *consider* it pure joy. It might not be all that great or enjoyable but consider it that way. It might not bring you any happiness at all in fact it might even ruin your entire year. No where does he say enjoy it. He says *consider* it pure joy. That makes it a little easier to understand. It reminds me of the dentist as he puts that enormously long needle in your mouth and says "this may sting a little at first but......" Why consider it joy? Because the testing of your faith develops perseverance. (testing, perseverance, trials ...can it get any more miserable than that?) What we all really want to hear is when it is all going to end? Not how we have to press on through it so we can build character. The truth is that there is relief and that what we have to endure is temporary as God never lets us have to deal with more than we are able to tackle. We just think we can't take anymore and really God is saying you are stronger than this and at the end of this journey you are going to be even stronger. As we are "tested" we grow. So why do we have to be tested? Why not skip all the test/trouble middle man and go right to the maturity of perseverance? Another key word missed. The testing of your faith *develops* perseverance. No other easier way around it. Sorry.

I have always been amazed by the determination of Olympian Athletes. Some even from young childhood train 6- 8 hours or even more daily to be able to have the skills and abilities they do as they perform. Many professional musicians are the same way. Practicing hours a day to be excellent at their craft. No other easier way around it. It involves discipline and determination. So how does perseverance in a Christian's life develop? Through trials. Through the testing of your faith. Perseverance is developed and makes you mature and complete not lacking in anything. Normally on any given day if you ask me if I'm spiritually mature, I'd say yes. I have room to grow but I feel mature. I have been a Christian since before I was a teenager and on top of that I have faced many tough situations before and pulled through miraculously. Many days I feel I have reached my quota of problems and think its time to spread it out a little. You know, share. In my mind I'm thinking that if my physical stamina was a visual model of my spiritual growth then Van Diesel would have some serious competition. But, *my* mind often plays a lot of tricks on me and I guess God has other things on *His* mind for me.

Spiritual growth is like no other growth. We've all had the Anatomy classes either in elementary or high school and have studied the human body at some time or another. Many of us have learned all the uniqueness of human growth and how we mature. The art and science to knowing how to grow in Christ though is not something that comes natural. Nor is it something you can read about or study in a text book. It takes hard work and dedication through a daily lifestyle. Just when you think you have grown up and jumped through all the hoops, there's more growing to do. It's an endless cycle. You never officially graduate from the school of "Christian Perfection". It is another opportunity to learn the essence of perseverance.

Perseverance I believe is one of the greatest challenges of the Christian walk and I know many of you would agree. It's easy to say I believe in God, I worship God, I live for God. But then actually doing it is a different story. Doing it while the world seems like it's caving in is even greater. It's like this huge wrestling match. I'm fighting to get up and walk away from it all and suddenly God puts me in a headlock and pins me down. I can hear the dialogue going something like this:

"I'm out of here"

"You're not going anywhere buddy"

'Ok. ok you got me. I give, I'll wait it out." (Then I try to make my fancy moves, get up and run away.) Bam. Sleeper hold. I'm down again.

My face to the floor I begin to notice I am far from the spiritual bodybuilder I thought I once was.

"I feel like I've been here before, when will the pain ever end?" Then God quotes those words of that verse in James. *"Perseverance must finish its work in you so that you may be mature and complete not lacking in anything."* I can picture God picking me up and holding me tightly again. And I simply say

"God, you want to loosen up a bit on the squeeze? I feel if I'm any closer to you one of us is going to choke or quit breathing or something." To which he replies…

"Come closer to me. You keep trying to slip away and I'm never going to let you go. Be strong and hang on. It will be tough but I have big plans for you. Really big and awesome plans. Just wait and see. You're never going to get a way."

Deeper

> *"The truth is that there is relief and that what we have to endure is temporary as God never lets us have to deal with more than we are able to tackle. We just think we can't take anymore and really God is saying you are stronger than this and at the end of this journey you are going to be even stronger"*

1. What things in your life are you wrestling with right now that make you feel like giving up?

2. Have you taken the time to offer these things to God in worship?

3. Take a moment and thank God for you any difficult circumstances you may be in right now and ask Him to help you learn the secret of perseverance through it all.

MY PRISON

"Set me free from my own prison,
that I may praise Your name"

Psalm 142:7

Solid steel bars, confined space, seclusion, alone, limitations, darkness, separation from the outside world. These are some words that come to mind when I hear the word prison. Ever feel trapped like you can't get away from your current life situation, your feelings, thoughts, heartaches, doubts and confusion? Do you want to move past all that so you can just feel normal again "get on with it"? King David with his gift of lyrical poetry was able to capture those exact feelings in this Psalm. Amazingly, still in the midst of those feelings he found himself worshipping God. Even when God seemed absent.

If there is anything that blocks us more from worship its personal struggle. It's not a natural human response to celebrate, praise and glorify anything when you feel trapped, used or hopeless. Ever thought about that? When someone cuts you off at an intersection have you ever just broke out in song? Probably not. When you find your account is overdrawn do you shout out "Praise the Lord!" Not me. Have you ever felt overwhelmed with Joy when a close relative died and start to dance down the hospital corridors? Or when your whole world seems like its caving in? It just doesn't seem natural to praise anything in a moment like that.

I remember being on my way to a new job about an hour away before and getting stuck in a major traffic jam that seemed to be uniquely arranged by someone to ruin my perfect plans of being on time. It was an important day and I was going to be late. I sat there trying to be patient and make due with my time. Still not moving. It was about 20 minutes later and right in the middle of this 8 lane highway I had a break down I couldn't take it anymore. I don't often get mad. Never at God. But I started yelling and I knew or at least thought God was the only person listening.

"Come on! I went out of my way to be on time today. Why does this have to happen? God help me out here. What's the deal? You trying to tell me something? Can you help me out maybe?" I hurt my voice. My arms were flyin. I'd love to see what I looked like. I was mad. To my embarrassment someone did see what I looked like. I'm in a traffic jam remember? Cars on both sides. No one is moving. What else is there to do but to look at other people around you? That's just what my fellow traffic jam neighbor was doing and what could be worse? My window was down. Whoops. Our eyes met. I went silent. He was staring at me looking down from his giant Peterbuilt cab. I was looking up at him and quickly cooling off in my little Chevy. I slowly rolled my eyes away for a second and began to think, got a quick idea, cranked my radio and tried to cover my actions by singing and dancing to the oldies. I'll be completely honest. I don't think he bought it. Not even for 3 seconds but it was at least worth the effort and the look on his face is one I'll never forget. Then just like clockwork the traffic miraculously starts to move again.

Stuck. Not one of my favorite feelings. In prison. Well I have been through one but never to stay. However, I have experienced a similar feeling. It's in those times though that we are given more than ever the opportunity to connect with the creator in worship in ways we never could have imagined. If we are able to connect with God in our times of being stuck and open our hearts to what He wants of us the situation reverses and we can find the power of freedom. If we were only able to look beyond the four walls that always try to hold us hostage and learn to step through the barriers we would be able to develop perseverance and find strength through anything. We just can't let go of the feeling of being stuck.

Tim Robbins in the movie *Shawshank Redemption* gives us the perfect example. Completely innocent he's put in prison for supposedly killing his wife. There he is confined in a prison cell for months at a time. Locked away with nothing but a few feet of space between four walls and darkness. Day after day, night after night all alone and waiting for that moment to be released. Alone with nothing but thoughts and memories in haunting him. Of course this was only a fictional story but it metaphorically paints the picture of what a lot of us often feel like. What keeps you going when you feel like you're at the end of your rope? How do you find encouragement to press on? In any situation like this you have a choice to make. You can either take advantage of the situation or let it get the best of you. If you remember in that movie if you have seen it, he makes the best of his time there making friends, finding support, offering learning opportunities to other inmates and financial assistance to the warden.

In this verse from the Psalms, we can see David in his distress called out to God trying to rise above the problem and into God's presence. Through all his heartache and pain he was asking God to meet him in a time of need and to release him from the bondage of life, the baggage of being human and to help him to again find the joy of worship. We all have our own "prisons" whether it's our guilt, shame, pride, the spirit of bitterness, sinful desires, etc, etc. Sometimes we choose to hold on to these things and remain in our cells. However God offers the key to being free again through complete surrender and trust in His name.

Why do we not want to be free of all that? We aren't really willing to let go and reach out. We are looking for a way of escape on our own. We look for a way to get out and continue living with those things that keep us locked up and stuck in a cycle that seems to never end. That's just the way we are. As long as we keep holding on to that baggage and have no trust in God we will remain in the 'stuck position". Because it's through those "stuck" times that God has our full attention and when he can finally take us, break us and make us into something more than we could ever imagine. We can bloom there into something greater than we ever knew we could. It's through the fire we are sharpened and made new. It's when we are stuck that God can finally make something of us. So my prayer is this, "Set us free God from the things that tie us down, from the things that keep us stuck and from worshipping you for all you are and from keeping us all that we need to be." Freedom comes when we worship God from our own "personal prisons".

Deeper

> *"If we are able to connect with God in our times of being stuck and open our hearts to what He wants of us the situation reverses and we can find the power of freedom."*

1. Have you ever felt completely stuck in a situation like you're not headed anywhere?

2. What does it mean to find freedom in Christ through praise & worship?

3. Try praising God the next time you find yourself in a predicament /dilemma of some-kind and see how it all works out.

BRAND NEW DAY

"Let the morning bring me word of Your unfailing love, for I have put my trust in You. Show me the way I should go for to You I lift up my soul."

Psalm 143:8

I remember the first time watching the movie "Ground Hogs Day" with Bill Murray and thinking wow this is so true. It's not only a classic favorite but often times we find ourselves actually living it. Each day his alarm would go off playing the same song and with the same news. Each day he would realize that it was just another repeat of the day before but with opportunities to either do something different with it or give up. He went through a phase of using this never ending cycle to his advantage and then a phase of wanting to end his own life due to the frustration or it all. It's the perfect example of how so many people live their lives. You get out of bed. Your feet hit the floor and each day is an exact repeat of the day before. Your life becomes mundane and you lose all passion to live.

Everyone goes through their routines getting ready for the day, going to their jobs, careers, vocations or whatever the case may be, dealing with schedules, demands, responsibilities and dealing with personal agendas. Sooner or later the work day is over you wind down and go through your evening "routines" crash in bed again only to find it starts all over again. On top of demands and schedules are the other surprises of life that cause stress and pain on top of all the pressure you already have. The passion sooner or later is gone as everything has sucked you dry and there is no more drive to keep you going. It's in these times that you begin to sink and give up losing all hope of a life full of adventure.

Every day is a gift from God. It's just what we do with it that really makes it more than "just another day". To break free from the cycle you have to know and answer the questions... What is your passion in life? What is it that makes you tick? What are you really living for? This verse in Psalm 143 is a great verse to help answer all those questions and kick off each day. It helps to put everything into perspective as soon as the alarm rings as every morning we again have another chance to have a fresh start at life.

The Psalmist one desire in this lyric is simply to hear the loving voice of God as soon as he awoke. He was overwhelmed by his own life and knew that God's love would rekindle his passion for living. At the crack of dawn Lord let your unfailing love shine brighter than the sun itself.

Sometimes getting out of bed in the morning seems to be the biggest task of the day as we dread all the things we have lined up and have to conquer before we can come home, mentally clock out and relax again. David knew the secret to make every second of the day full of pleasure and satisfaction. Forget about fueling up on that quadruple shot vanilla Latte. No over the counter drug can compete with a life that is filled with passion and has a genuine desire to live for Jesus. Jesus is the reason we have each new day and by connecting with him we can find new life, new energy and a new purpose for each and every day. The antidote for your repetitive, mundane lifestyle is the love of God that brings passion back to your soul and begins to flow through your bloodstream with side effects that are amazingly, positively and ridiculously powerful.

The first thought that might run through your mind when hearing that a passion for living for Jesus can change your whole lifestyle might be "ok so how in the world does that work?" For a non-believer this may sound even like a cultish philosophy or some kind of mind- altering technique. It does come across as sci-fi or even un-realistic but for many of us who have experienced it as Christians it is nothing but amazing. There is no experiment or scientific theology to explain it. It's just the way we're wired. God's unfailing love gives us a change of pace. It breaks up the monotony and provides something new. You can get so wrapped up in it that it will leave you in wonder and a new outlook. It's like that relationship you have in your life with that special someone. You know the person you enjoy spending so much time with. When you are together you are consumed in the moment and wrapped up in the other person. Everything around you that before was dark, painful or even boring seems to disappear.

Passion comes from a relationship that is alive and active. God's love still remains even though yesterday is gone. God's love still remains after today is gone. In that alone you can discover His faithfulness and trust in Him. It's the only thing that remains consistent. Every morning we have an opportunity to come before God and ask for guidance in everything we do and say. Taking advantage of that opportunity will uncover the change you've been looking for in your life. Grab a hold of the Love of God and it will change the way you live. David in this Psalm shows how he starts off the day worshipping God as he asks God for his wisdom and has offers his life as a tool. What do you want of me today? Where do I go from here? We have our own personal goals but real passion in life comes from that simple spark we receive from the love of God. No matter what may be going on in your life either good or bad after reading this verse in Psalm 143 it helps set the focus for the outcome of the entire day. It helps you to refocus on what life is all about.

Every morning we are reminded of God's faithfulness and love for creation just by the fact that there is another day to live. The least we can do is ask the creator for insight on now we can live to the fullest each day we have been given. When that happens regularly you will never be the same as you will be blessed with a restored passion, a life full of adventure and new purpose. No more mundane daily routines. It's a brand new day with a million opportunities to discover the passion of an everlasting love, of an everlasting God.

Deeper

> *"Passion comes from a relationship that is alive and active. God's love still remains even though yesterday is gone. God's love still remains after today is gone. In that alone you can discover His faithfulness and trust in Him."*

1. Have you ever spent the first part of you day in worship?

2. What is it that drives and motivates you on a daily basis?

3. Have you ever stopped to listen to the voice of God in your busy schedule?

CHAPTER 4:

FAITH:
THE DEEP END OF THE OCEAN

I admit it. I as a child was one of the proud and few to have my very own Stretch Armstrong. You know the toy. That little, muscular, rubber blonde man filled with some kind of liquid that allows him to stretch and eventually go back to his original shape. Just as any kid, I stretched that little man to death pulling his arms, legs and his head with that huge smiley toothsome grin, as far as I could. Often I would ask a friend or someone else to help pull on one end as I yanked on the other just to see how far he could really go. Although I never broke this crazy toy I felt I often came very close. I always found myself turning my head when I was pulling him to protect myself from his possible bodily explosion of super stretchy juice or whatever it was that made him so amazingly flexible. Sometimes when I think of my old toy, Stretch Armstrong I think of how I feel when I am being stretched in my faith. Faith as you know is believing in something that can't be seen or trusting in something that seems impossible. It's being moved to new limits. To me as strange childish as it may seem, Stretch illustrated that point perfectly in many different ways.

Faith in different situations can stretch us to impossible ends. If you thought your faith was pretty strong already, stop right there. It will be stretched even more. Through trials, struggles, pain, heartache and suffering it will take you to the point where you feel so stretched out your going to explode. Luckily your arms and legs can only go so far. What is stretched with faith is stuff on the inside. It's painful and random. It will stretch and pull you with no remorse. Then it might let go or try stretching you in a whole new way. That's how it works. It takes you past the point of no return. Past what we would automatically know, believe, trust and have faith in and helps you to find faith in so much more beyond that. Faith also builds a trust in the unknown.

Faith in general, to me seems like one of the most misunderstood, most generally used and most forgotten integral part of Christianity. I have to admit I have been a believer, a regular church at tender and have learned about faith ever since I was able to first say the word but I am still learning exactly what it is and how it works everyday thirty some years later. It doesn't hit you and filtrate through you like a lightening bolt and then automatically become part of your lifestyle. It builds up over time and is daily challenged and strengthened.

Faith according to Easton's Bible dictionary has been defined as ... "the persuasion of the mind that a certain statement is true. A primary idea is true therefore worthy of trust." Evidence leads you to believe in it and its reliability and consistency. It's longer lasting than a Duracell battery, more solid then a steel wall more dependable than the air you breathe. We can choose to believe and trust in something but again our faith in that idea or object is tested daily. To fully understand faith and trust in God it involves personal experience. An experience that involved scripture and life situations. When you begin your own personal journey to completely understanding faith and use it daily through all seasons you will recognize its amazing power and wonder how you ever lived without it.

The Pavlov Experiment

Remember studying a guy named Pavlov in high school? The name is hard to forget. I love that name. Say it out loud. Pavlov. When you hear the name Pavlov, does it ring a bell? (pun intended) If not let me give you some other clues. Drooling dogs, classical conditioning. OK this might all sound very strange but let me explain what I'm trying to get at here. Pavlov was a Russian physiologist popular for his study in animal behaviors leading to major breakthroughs for Psychology. You most likely have run across this name somewhere in your studies in high school or college. Whatever the case let me give you a short crash course on the idea of classical conditioning that he discovered. Ivan Pavlov had been studying the digestive tracks of dogs when he first noticed the conditional process. He would place a morsel of food on the dogs tongue to get them to salivate. Not too long after he first started this experiment he noticed they would salivate even before being presented with food. Sometimes drooling when he entered the room or even when they heard him coming down the hall. In his study then salivation was recognized as a reflex. A natural reflex.

This guy actually made money studying dog drool. On top of that he was passionate about it and learned new things as he studied this behavior everyday. He wanted to study the possibility of a natural reflex being affected by learning. Using a bell that he referred to as a neutral stimulus he began to think through how to condition their behavior. Bell rings. Dogs could care less. Then he would feed the dogs. Scientifically speaking, food was the stimulus leading to drool, the response. You still with me here? OK I know it sounds a bit gross and irrelevant but believe me there is a point to this even if I have to make one up. Here is where the conditioning comes in. After he repeated this event soon the dogs would start to salivate when hearing the bell. Bell rings. Dogs drool. The bell now was the conditioned stimulus leading to the conditioned response. From a dog's perspective… Ding dong, Alpo, drool everywhere.

Drool, Dogs, Salivation and Faith

Drool, dogs, salivation and bells. What does this have to do with faith or worship? Good question. When I was reminded of the Pavlov experiment it made me think of some similar ways faith works. If you could imagine with me the whole idea of conditioning. Just as the dogs began salivating when food was present or the thought of food entered their brain, faith should be our conditioned response we have learned from a God who remains faithful in every way through eternity.

Here's my proposal. Let's try this. Put suffering and crisis and heartache and all that painful jazz into the place of the conditioned stimulus. Faith will be the conditioned response. What do you think that would look like?   Heartache enters, Faith leaks out. Imagine how deep your faith would be if this could happen. Heartache is something we face quite often. Faith could grow and become greater than any problem that comes your way. It's the same with the idea of worship. Again with pain and struggles being our conditioned stimulus replace the response with worship. Crisis steps in, worship flows out. Despair steps in, worship flows out. Get the picture? If we could learn how to replace the negative with the positive and to turn a rainstorm into an opportunity to dance we would find ourselves sinking deeper into the heart of our God. We would learn how to find a worship opportunity out of any circumstance.

Lost

Instead we are overwhelmed with a feeling like were stranded out in the middle of an ocean. We feel lost at sea. You are barely holding on while that little voice still cries out.

"Give up. Give in. No one is going to save you. No one cares. God doesn't need your worship right now. You have yourself to take care of."

You have been treading water, calling out for help, fighting to stay alive and still no response. No answer. No hope. It's so much easier to give up and think all is lost when everything seems hopeless then to have a little faith that you aren't going to drown. Have you ever been lost before? I mean really lost? I mean like the wandering aimlessly around the backwoods of a National Forest kind of lost. Or the driving in circles in downtown New York City kind of lost. Being lost is an awkward feeling. Especially when you have no map, no directions, no idea of where to go or what could happen. Most likely you have felt lost before and you know exactly what I'm talking about.

What about being lost from God? Ever felt like that? Have you ever felt like you are in a place where God can not hear you, see you or help? You might be thinking what in the world is God up to now? What is this all about? What do I do next? Where do I go? Amazingly though in our spiritual journey sometimes we have to be lost to be truly found. It's when we have no where left to turn or go that God can catch us dead in our tracks and take control. It's through rough waters that we are put to the test and we can see how deep our faith really is.

Several years ago I was going through one of those times in my life when I wrote the words for this song called *Sweet Love*.

I was drifting out in the ocean, with no sign of life for miles away
There's no sail or compass here to guide me,
there's no way to tell the time of day.
Only one thing to be sure of. As the sky turns to shades of grey.
I know Your all around me. And it gives
me strength to face another day.

Chorus:
It's your love, sweet love that came and save me.
It's your love, sweet love that rescued me
I was feeling oh so very weary, Lost in a world only in my mind
I was searching for all the answers, but the
questions seem to be all that I find.
They say what won't kill you, makes you stronger
But right now I'm feeling torn apart
There's a cure and there's an answer and I found it in Your heart

Chorus:
It's your love, sweet love that came and saved me
It's your love, sweet love that rescued me

In my search to figure it all out for myself I again found Jesus. In my attempt to save myself I found the only way to be saved was to let go of everything I held on to and grab on to God. Completely drained of all my own selfish ambitions and feeble attempts at trying to stay afloat I began to sink to the bottom of the ocean while my spiritual self was raised to walk on water. I was not alone at all but found that God was with me the entire time waiting until I had nothing left to hold on to but God himself. All old was gone and the new had come. At that moment all hope was found and faith restored. I wish I could say that I remained strong each and every time I have been challenged in my spiritual life ever since then but I can't. Each time though I find myself stronger and without reason to doubt. It's in those moments that we all have our chances to go deeper into the love of God. Throughout the Bible from front to back you can stories of individuals who were challenged and taken out of their comfort zones to bring them to a new place in life. Most were faithful through all seasons of difficulty and one of my favorites, being a worship leader and musician myself is King David.

The Faithful Worshipper

David was a man of faith. However way you look at it you have to realize his faith was strong and deep. Among all faithful men and women of the Bible he stands out to me simply because he was a worshipper in all seasons. That alone to me speaks volumes. He makes it evident in every song he wrote and every word he included. In times of excitement and in times of desperation you can see how he constantly turned to God. What an awesome sight and amazing sound it must have been to see David sitting there with his harp in hand playing music and singing such beautiful, poetic and meaningful lyrics and heartfelt response to his creator.

Imagine yourself with a character like David, in a more modern setting. Just sitting there in the beauty of God's world, with your guitar singing praise to God. Singing whatever came to mind in adoration of the King. Rhyme scheme or not. Simply putting words from your soul to a tune to express yourself. As we had discussed in the previous chapters the Psalms are often thought as praises to God when a vast majority of them are really songs crying out in desperation for God to help in time of need. David knew his God was faithful to hear, listen and respond and he continually through the good and the bad communicated with the Savior through his music. There is nowhere else to turn when it comes to dependability in times of need other than God himself. He remains today and forever the same. The words and praise of David's heart written for us today in the music of the Psalms are an awesome example to follow as we search to find ways to worship God while struggling through each day.

Music in itself as we know is a powerful tool. It's even more powerful as it is used to worship God, as David knew and experienced throughout his life. Armies under his reign used it on the forefront as they entered into battle to build confidence. He used it to calm the worries and fears of the King himself and through his art used it to express himself in his search for knowing God, to build his faith and calm his own personal fears. Speaking of fear….

Fear Factor

The greatest enemy of Faith's is fear itself. It's fear of the unknown and even fear of losing control of life as we know it. Faith is security. Faith is trust. Faith is sitting back and watching the impossible literally happens right in front of your eyes. We don't want to let go of our lives and let God do His thing because we don't know what will happen next. It might be something outside our comfort zone that we aren't ready for or willing to do. Of course it would be easy if we knew what God was going to do as it may make us a bit less reluctant to let go of it all. But that wouldn't be faith. Many of us, including myself, would still not want to let go due to our human nature. Look at what happened to Peter. He did know before he got out of the boat what God was going to do for him and in fear after he was walking on water began to sink. Walking on water he lost his faith. Not while getting out of the boat. We might not know what lies up ahead if we walk in faith but we will know the promise that God is with us along the way. Check out what Isaiah says.

"Fear not for I have redeemed you, I have summoned you by name. You are mine. When you pass through the waters I will be with you. And when you pass through the rivers they will not sweep over you when you walk through the fire you will not be burned. The flames will not set you ablaze." Isaiah 43:1-2

I will be with you. Words straight from the heart of God. A simple promise that we can hold on to. Fear interrupts faith from blossoming into a full trust in God. God only wants us to have faith and nothing less. If we live in fear and not in faith we are saying, we don't believe God can take care of us. It's like saying "Yah God, You're in control but I'm not 100% sure yet so maybe

I'll give you the driver's seat next time around." Face it, fear is nothing but dead weight. Letting it go is the best thing you could ever do. Drop the fear that weighs you down and hold on to the faith that keeps you afloat.

Real Faith

Ok. Here we are. This is where "the rubber meets the road". Where reality starts to kick in. This is where real faith in God is found. We have questioned God and been angry. So what's next God? Do you have a plan? You have brought me this far and I have trusted you to this point now are you just going to leave me here? Now we along the path find ourselves praying the same prayer David prayed as he wrote.

"The Lord will fulfill His purpose for me, Your love O Lord endures forever do not abandon the works of your hands."

The bottom line is you have to let go of everything that might hinder you from going deeper into the abyss of the ocean that leads into the awesome of God's love. We have cried out to God. He has heard. Now we have to wait and trust. It's the final stage. The final moment where we finally admit out loud

"I can't do this anymore. Take all of me."

"What was that?" He asks

"That's right God I have faith and trust in you to take all of me and do your thing. I'm done being in control and trying to figure it out on my own. I want to sink deep into your ultimate will for my life."

Once you come to this point I can see that smile that breaks out across the face of God as He begins to prepare us for the next step. When we finally recognize God in all His faithfulness we are just beginning to see the phenomenal things he will be able to do from here on out with our lives. He's shaping you into his perfect plan. God's faithfulness has extended from the very beginning of creation to this very second you are reading this sentence and He has no reason to stop now. His goal is to develop a similar strong and long-lasting faith in us even if it takes longer then we ever had planned.

Have faith in God. When God seems far away, have faith in God. When you are feeling trapped, have faith in God. When I can't take anymore and feel like I'm going to go ballistic, have faith in God. Personally I don't like being stretched past my limits but if it brings me closer to God and deeper into his love then I am all for it. Sign me up. Stretch me and pull me until I'm so out of shape that I'm not even recognizable anymore. Stretch me into something new.

Time To Be Stretched

OK, I have another confession. I did get another Stretch Armstrong since I was a child. I think I actually got it while in college. The first one was lost or was sold at a yard sale or something like that. It's a great toy for all ages you know. As a kid you can torment the guy and stretch him for fun. He can take it. As an adult you can stretch the heck out of him and relieve some stress. I did enjoy it for quite a while and had him up until about 5 years ago. In that time frame my kids got a hold of him and soon he was lost in a giant mountain of toys in their play room. So needless to say he wasn't stretched for quite a while. Mr. Armstrong was finally getting his long awaited break from his curse of lifelong torture and deformity. I personally think he stayed hiding in that pile as long as he could trying to protect himself from people like me.

I wish I had kept better track of him though because I found him a year or two later after my family had moved to a new home. There he was packed away in the bottom of a box. Still smiling away and showing off his golden locks of hair. To my surprise he was very un-flexible and stiff as a board. What had happened? Was this the same Stretch I had known, loved and played with so many times before? Maybe his magical stretch

Faith: The Deep End of the Ocean

potion had worn off. Maybe he had expired? Then I started to think. Maybe it was the stretching that was keeping him alive. Maybe it was the stretching that made him who he was meant to be. After all that was his name and if your first name is Stretch you have a lot to live up to. So my question for you is…are you willing to be stretched before you become completely hardened?

FAITH ILLUSTRATED

"Now faith is being sure of what we hope for and certain of we do not see."

Hebrews 11:1

No need to go and dig out your Webster's Dictionary. Right here in Hebrews in black and white God has defined the word faith in the most simple of words. Sure of what we hope for and certain of what we don't see. Pretty amazing stuff. Let's try an experiment ok? Go to your car and start it up. If you literally can't go to your car right now that's fine. Just pretend. Are you ready? Ok step number one make sure it's in the off position. You are sure of what will happen when you turn the key right? If everything is working right your engine will purr like a kitten. You are certain of it even though it hasn't happened yet. So turn the key and see what happens.

- The engine starts up and starts running (You can do your Tim Allen Grunt here)
- Turn it off and try again.....
- Oh yeah the sound of small explosions in the piston chamber starts again.
- Turn it off

This is how simple faith in things works. There is evidence it will work. It has worked many other times in this same way and will as long as every part is in place and is working properly.

Or how about this. Go to your fridge. OK you know what sits behind that door. You have seen it before. A half drank gallon of milk, leftover pizza from last night, a bag of grapes, some cold cuts, maybe some vegetables so on and so on. Then you remember that last slice of chocolate pie you were saving for later and with high expectations of it still being there you open the door. It's gone!! My first guess is that you haven't lost faith in your refrigerator or in the whole refrigeration industry. You most likely would figure someone had gotten there before you and eaten it. Thus the reason it's no longer there. It's at this point I'm guessing and have faith (if you are like me) that you will now be a on mission to hunt this person down and make sure this situation will never happen again. Faith is something we practice everyday in many ways. Take these situations for example.

- You wake up in the morning and look at your clock. You have faith the time is correct.
- You turn on the light and have faith the room will be illuminated.
- You go to the bathroom and turn on the water. You have faith water will flow from the pipes.
- You breathe in each breath having faith that when you exhale you can take another breath all over again.

All day long every day the faith/belief system is working. You experience it in some way or another everyday. I have faith right now as I type on my computer that every stroke of a key is going to put a new word on the screen and eventually print on paper. I type it and there it is. I continue typing and it continues showing up. Still typing, Words are still showing up.

Now let's take the faith thing a little further. Don't worry this won't hurt. We have faith in small things and don't even notice. For example the things I just mentioned. However, it's when it comes to having faith God that it seems to be a problem. Faith is knowing something is dependable and trustworthy. It's reliable and proven. People can be dependable and reliable but often times fail. We are often times un-faithful in our commitments, un-faithful in our relationships and un-faithful in our promises. A clock can faithfully tell time (unless it's broken or powerless) because that's what it was made to do. Faithfulness to us is a choice. We have the ability to be faithful but don't always choose to be that way. Faith is not as easy to practice as it is to define.

Faith in God is even more difficult. Especially since it involves belief in something not physically visible, touchable or audible. Faith in things of this world are completely meaningless when compared to faith in something as great as God. Even though it's difficult, faith in God is what gives you true hope and peace and life. Everyone knows faith in the things of this world will get you no where. God is the only thing that is always reliable, dependable and trustworthy. He never breaks down, runs out of power or chooses to be faithless. He can't. It's what makes him God. The only thing is you can't see Him. You can however see his power in action if you want your "proof ". Let's try another experiment.

- Think about a time when a crisis came into your life. You prayed and looked to God for the answers. He provided, blessed and protected you. You came out on the other side of it in pretty good shape.
- Think of another time when a crisis came into your life. You prayed and worshipped and looked to God for the answers. He provided, blessed and protected you. You came out of it knowing again that God was with you all the way.
- Ok now you are facing heartache in life. You prayed and looked to God for the answers and wait. You remember how God provided, blessed and protected you before.
- You continue to pray and look to God and wait. You know God will pull you through somehow and you continue to wait and pray.
- Repeat steps as necessary.

Deeper

> *"God is the only thing that is always reliable, dependable and trustworthy. He never breaks down, runs out of power or chooses to be faithless. He can't. It's what makes him God. The only thing is you can't see Him. You can however see his power in action."*

1. On a scale from 1-10 (10 being the highest) how strong is your faith in God at this moment?

2. Why do you think our faith often changes?

3. Does worship and continual focus on God help build faith? Why do you think that way? How does it work?

AUTHOR OF FAITH

"Let us fix our eyes on Jesus, the author and perfector of our faith who for the joy set before him endured the cross scorning its shame and sat down at the right hand of the throne of God. Consider Him who endured such opposition from sinful men, so that you will not grow weary and lose heart."

Hebrews 12:2-3

I remember the first time I saw the first episode of Lord of the Rings. I actually had no idea it was the first of a trilogy. Call me blonde but I didn't have a clue. I'm not sure how I missed out on I'm not sure how I missed out on that key information but I did. So I went to see it with high expectations and a lot of anticipation of adventure. Then all that amazing storyline and intense drama came to an end. Slam on the brakes. Over. Done. No conclusion. No bad guy gets defeated. No memorable punch line. Just a scenic shot of the mountains and the credits role. I was quite disappointed. I left feeling like I had just spent three hours to be left hanging. The best part of the movie though is that that wasn't the end of the story. As a matter of fact there is not just another three hour sequel but a third. You just had to wait another year. The story does go on. There is an end. There's two more parts of the series to follow and everything that is left undone will come to the perfect conclusion at the end of the trilogy in the Return of the King.

I imagine anyone who experienced the life of Jesus first hand must have felt the same way. All his life was full of amazing events and intense dramatic stories and then it all came to a screeching halt. Over. Done. No real conclusion. The bad guys are not defeated. The good guy is left hanging, literally. The crowds were left hanging, mentally. To both theirs and our surprise though this was just the first part of the trilogy. The life and death of Christ. The life He lived was spent setting the standard for faithfulness. He remained faithful through every crisis that came his way in order to fulfill the mission he was sent to complete. For the joy on the other side, which is experienced in part two and three, he endured the cross and all the hell that went with it.

Many people who experienced Jesus ministry, the ultimate example of a lifestyle of faith, missed the whole reason why He lived. That was to tell about the conclusion of the story he was living. To share with the multitudes his faithful promise to come again and take them into a place far greater than they could ever imagine. To their dismay they only saw the first of the trilogy. As a matter of fact only 40 or so saw the second part, the resurrection and ascension into heaven and many of them were still confused and didn't believe.

Jesus is the author and perfector of our faith. He created it. He designed it and helps us to develop it until it comes full circle to its fullest potential. If we focus on him and worship Him for all He is, He will help us to know, truly believe and trust in all of his ways. Even when they don't make sense. Even when they may leave us hanging for weeks, months or even years. Through our trust in God we find that there is conclusion and an end to all the chaos that goes on beforehand. The answers to our confusion and doubt lie on the other side of the fence where you find true faith.

There are many times when your faith is tried in the hardships and you only wish for some quick answer or result. The whole crucifixion story and events leading toward it were more of a hardship then anything any human should have to live through. Knowing He could have bailed at any given second and escaped all the torture, yet didn't, is mind-boggling. We have seen the vulgarity of what He went through in Mel Gibson's Passion movie. Yet as it says here "for the joy set before him he endured the cross". That is a pretty big eye-popping, jaw-dropping, heart-stopping joy. Through his death he knew He could conquer all that junk, the pain and suffering we endure daily, for everyone and for all time. That's the joy that was set before him. With faith we too can find hope and joy that we will never have to suffer in anyway anymore and we will again find the passion for continuous worship. Sure our heartache seems overwhelming but not in the shadow of what Jesus endured on the cross. Of course it doesn't mean what we are suffering is nothing. The cross only helps to put it all our daily suffering into a different perspective. A bad day or even week is a hard comparison to the scene of the cross.

His commitment to faith through the pain, through the cross, through the mocking and pressure opened the door to give us a way out from it all. Sure we have to wade through all of it for now but not forever. That's where part three comes in. The author of our faith is also the author of the story of life, the author of part one and two and the sequel to it all. Pain doesn't last forever. Doubt, confusion and despair are temporary. Your faith is being made stronger everyday as you sort through whatever comes your way. Just know that it will not last forever but you will.

As God builds our faith we build character and hope knowing that He will walk with us along the way. Part one and two of the series was pretty awesome. Part three of the trilogy is the one we spend a lifetime waiting for. *The Return of the King*. Through the whole thing our faith continues to develop towards perfection and our worship for him becomes more intense. We *know* of Jesus life and death. We *believe* in his resurrection. Now comes the last part of the process that is painful. Trust. Trusting that he will give us hope every day to find strength to go through the trials. Trusting that he will return soon so we at some point won't have to deal with it anymore. Want to know how real faith works and how this life-story is going to come to conclusion? Get to know the author.

Deeper

"Jesus is the author and perfector of our faith. He created it. He designed it and helps us to develop it until it comes full circle to its fullest potential. If we focus on him and worship Him for all He is, He will help us to know, truly believe and trust in all of his ways"

1. What are some things that keep you from fixing your eyes on Jesus daily?

2. How does this verse give you hope in dealing with challenges you may have in your life presently?

3. Take a moment and worship God for all He has done for you in your life.

BLIND-SPOT

"For our Struggle is not against flesh and blood but against the rulers, against the authorities, against the powers of this dark world and against the spiritual forces of evil in the heavenly realms. Therefore put on the full armor of God so that when the day of evil comes you may be able to stand your ground."
" Take up the shield of faith with which you can extinguish all the flaming arrows of the evil one."

Ephesians 6:12-13 & 16

Sometimes I wonder what the auto industry was thinking when they designed cars with something as dangerous and crazy as a blind-spot. Call me nuts but the words drive and blind shouldn't even go together. Should they? I don't know about you but when I get behind the wheel of my vehicle I want to know exactly what's in front of me, what's behind me and what's going on, on both sides. We have safety belts, air bags, alarms, anti theft systems and all sorts of protective devices but hey, if you get up in my blind-spot just forget it, you will get nailed. You have no way to tell what's going on. Dangerous or not. Hopefully you know what a blind spot in a car is but if not let me explain. It's generally the area on the side of the car between your rear view mirror and side mirror where you have no vision. The area where none of your mirrors reflect what's going on. It's the danger zone.

I have many times been surprised by something that happened in my blind-spot that could have been tragic but got lucky and was able to manage.

Speaking of blind spots let me tell you about one that everyone has and often doesn't even realize. Its better know as the spiritual realm, which this verse descriptively talks about. Right now Hollywood, more than ever, has been focusing on this topic that everyone used to believe was imaginary and totally un-believable. Hollywood has made a huge market out of shows and movies that focus on this particular theme. All give a picture of something more out there other than humanity and ideas of spiritual worlds but they do not even come even close to hitting the mark of what the Spirit World really consists of. Believe-able or not the truth is, it does exist. The spirit world is out there. If you ever wondered why you are struggling at times or even dealing with something that is more powerful than you (addictions, emotional instability, physical disabilities, etc) there just might be more to it. Satan himself can attack you through the spirit world causing heartache and grief in every way imaginary. It's evident through the story of Job as we looked at earlier in chapter one. Satan had actually asked permission from God if he could torment Job's life and then sent his followers to carry out his wicked scheme. (Job 1:6-12.) You can't see it going on but it's there.

If somehow we were able to see this "blind-spot", this spirit world around us, we would no doubt add a whole new level to our understanding of what life is really about. There's an invention to be created and patented. Spirit world goggles that you can slip on and that give you the whole inside view. Kind of like night vision goggles but twenty-four seven. No more "spiritual blind-spot". Talk about freaky. Just being able to somehow see this other dimension happening around us firsthand and in literal form would be an instant reality check. Through the power of the Holy Spirit we are able to do just that. To see beyond the ordinary world around us and get a glimpse at reality. Something deeper. Something more. It takes us deeper into faith and deeper into God.

Our struggles and suffering not only come from the present world we live in but from the outer world of the heavenly realms just as much. That is why there is so much more to what is going on in our lives then what meets the eye. Even though it's in our blind-spot we have to trust and have faith in God that He will defend us when we are in danger. Through faith we are given the strength to know we can make it through the battles that engage around us and that God will protect us from harm as we journey through. This verse includes the armor of God which uses the metaphor of armor to symbolize how to find protection from the evil one including the shield of faith that keeps us from being destroyed.

Personally I find myself struggling with Satan's attacks every single day. Doubt, confusion, frustration and anger keep raging on and I often want to cash in on all the things I've stood for, for so long. On top of that I often find Him at times trying to steal my passion for worship. He knows that's a huge part of me and when he steals a passion like that anything can happen. Some days I feel I was personally selected for target practice and I'm about to drop to my knees and surrender. Then I remember to use my shield. The shield of faith that keeps Satan's arrows from piercing us straight into the heart. It's not literal of course but it often feels like it. I don't normally carry around a huge metal protective device or wear a bulletproof vest. Satan can penetrate right through that kind of stuff anyway. That kind of stuff only protects from the outside in. Satan's best defense is from the inside out. I have to keep reminding myself to stand firm in my faith. Let that protect me from anything that happens and when I may least expect it to happen.

Just like anyone I like to see what's going on around me at all times. I like to be informed of danger just in case I need to take cover. For example a red engine light. Better pull over my engine is over heating. "Head's Up" better look something is falling from the sky and it's headed your way. "Duck" Stay low, you're about to get walloped. But for the worst danger of all the danger that happens in our "blind-spot" there is no real warning call or advance notice of trouble. Just the simple words, "have faith". It may not seem like a lot but your faith in a time of struggle when war is raging all around you, when heavenly forces are attacking the dark world, when heaven & hell are being battling it out in your blind-spot, its really all you need and all you have to defend yourself. Have faith and never lose sight of the one you worship. Truth is that's really all we need, whether you can see what's really happening around you or not.

Deeper

> *"Even though it's in our blind-spot we have to trust and have faith in God that He will defend us when we are in danger. Through faith we are given the strength to know we can make it through the battles that engage around us and that God will protect us from harm as we journey through."*

1. What kinds of spiritual battles are you facing right now?

2. Have you found yourself caught in the middle of a spiritual battle that weighed on you very heavy?

3. How can worshipping our creator help you see the spiritual battle that's going on around you?

TELL ME HOW, TELL ME NOW

"Do not be anxious about anything but in everything, by prayer and petition, with thanksgiving present your requests to God. And the peace of God which transcends all understanding, will guard your hearts and your minds in Christ Jesus"

Philippians 4:6-7

Do not be anxious about anything? I only have two words in response to that phrase. "Yeah right." Reality check. How in the world are we expected to ignore all anxiety and stress that comes our way? It doesn't seem normal or even human to think anyone can just sit back relax believing that everything is just going to work out on its own. It's just not right. It's not how were wired. You would have to pretty abnormal to have a personality like that.

"What did you say? The checking account is way overdrawn again? Ah no worries. It will all balance out sometime."

"Did you say you're having some major heart problems again? Oh well nothing last forever, ya know?"

"I just got a phone call from the in-laws and they have to move in with us for the next couple years. This is going to be awesome!"

Anxiety happens to all of us. Ignoring it sounds practically impossible. However if we could only see the whole picture in advance then maybe it would be a little easier. You know like

100

a private advanced screening of your own life story on the big screen with large buttered popcorn, a 32 ounce soda and a big box of Dots to go along with it. The bottom line is no matter what we think, we can't make it through life without a little stress or anxiety. We also can't deal with problems that come our way on our own. It's not how we were created. It's not the way we were designed. From my limited perspective I remain confused and overwhelmed about this even though my whole life I have been taught and told that God will work it all out, don't worry. Just have a little faith. But every ounce of humanness is yelling out

"But I want to know how and I want to know now!"

"This is my life and I want to be in charge!"

You might be able to relate to this when reading this verse at first or if you have ever had to wait on God. Let's break it down and think this through and I promise after we look at this closer you will understand how this verse can change your life. First of all, even though at first it doesn't seem right, you have to realize that in these words there is a ton of wisdom, power and answers that you can only find once you really study it. Take a closer look at what it says "Do not be anxious about anything, but in everything by prayer and petition and with thanksgiving present your requests to God". Ok I like that part. I have a lot of worry and stress and now at least I can present these concerns to God. That takes off some pressure. I don't have to ignore the issues but I can know that I don't have to deal with it all by myself. I can present them to God and I don't have to freak out about it. In God I can find a peace as I bring these things before Him. But the phrase "with thanksgiving" is tricky. What does that mean? I have to be thankful for the situation I am presenting? *Or is it* maybe just being thankful for the ability to come before God and present it to Him? Here after considering the options I would have to vote for option number two. Once you really read the words written in this text it all starts to make complete sense. So "in prayer and petition" (meaning to ask or even beg) I come before God offering these things in thanksgiving to Him. So if you really think about it, no matter how bad the situation is, there is always something to be thankful for as you don't have to deal with it yourself and can bring it before God Almighty. Even if it's embarrassing or painful. It's also good to have someone to spill your guts to. Someone safe where you can spill out your junk and re-fill back up with encouragement.

Then comes the best part to me that just blew me away. Check this out, it says, "The peace of God that transcends all understanding". Wow! The peace of God. I can't even begin to imagine what that's like but it says if I bring these requests before Him, He will in return give me a glimpse of it. Think about that. A peace of God. A total satisfaction or resolve that is so great it transcends anything we can imagine. It is un-comprehendable. It's unfathomable. Not only that but he also says it will "guard your heart and mind". Two major guarantees for just the asking! So what is being said here is just GIVE IT UP! Drop it at His feet. Offer it to him and He will provide complete peace and rest. Let it go and let God do what He is truly good at. Being God! God is always faithful to His word. God always is faithful to provide for His people who find rest in Him.

I tell you that after I read this verse again and again it started to make more sense and just what I needed to hear. Just like any other person on this planet I can only go so long without feeling like I'm going to snap when I'm under a lot of pressure. However, even if I don't know what is going to happen next or what tomorrow holds I at least can be at rest about it and not go crazy in the meantime. That's my biggest concern. My sanity. Sanity is a good thing, Insanity, not so cool. We have enough of that in the world already. Sure I might be able to muddle through on my own somehow but if I find myself on the other end drooling profusely, twitching violently and shouting out random animal names at everyone who passes by I think it would be pretty obvious that something is definitely wrong. Trust in God brings peace. That in itself makes the world seem a little simpler.

Replacing our anxiety with trust is difficult since we hold on to it so closely. That first step of faith can be awkward but before you know it you will be walking more confidently each step of the way.

These words were the perfect cure for my severe case of anxiety and I'm pretty sure it can bring peace to anyone who understands it and follows through. I took it and copied it and posted it in different places in my house. Now I can be reminded daily that I can find total peace in God if I just pray and not worry about what is in store. It's walking by faith. No vision necessary. Just know for a fact that God is going to take care of you no matter what tomorrow holds or where you end up. I re-read this verse whenever I can to know that I still need to trust God and I know sooner or later He's going to pull through for me. When will that be? I don't know. What does God have in store for me next? I have no clue. When will I understand his exact will and timing? Hopefully someday soon. Maybe never. How in the world can I find peace in a time of extreme pressure? Well it's simple. Convert your worries and fears into a prayer. Give Him praise and all your anxiety will evaporate into thin air. Offer up your prayer request and let God take care of the rest. It beats having to go to the Doctor, it's easier than taking medication, it's less time consuming than going to therapist, it doesn't leave you bloated or with a severe case of diarrhea, you get to keep your sanity and best of all its free.

I don't have all the answers but I don't have to be anxious for them. In this verse we are simply told how to find peace when we're ready to break and if I follow through by bringing my concerns and worries before God I can find instant relief. In the meantime now that I better understand what this verse is saying I honestly keep finding more peace everyday. More peace everyday with faith leading the way. On top of that it takes your worship of Him to a whole new level that will be more powerful than ever.

Deeper

> *"Give Him praise and all your anxiety will evaporate into thin air. Offer up your prayer request and let God take care of the rest. It beats having to go to the Doctor, it's easier than taking medication, it's less time consuming than going to therapist, it doesn't leave you bloated or with a severe case of diarrhea, you get to keep your sanity and best of all its free. "*

1. What kinds of things are causing you a lot of anxiety right now?

2. Have you brought these things before Him and dropped them at His feet?

3. If you haven't take a moment to do that now. If you have given Him thanks for that opportunity you had to come before Him and give Him praise for what He is doing.

IT ALL WORKS OUT
IN THE END

*"And we know that in all things God works
for the good of those who love him who have
been called according to his purpose."*

Romans 8:28

I love the movie "The Incredibles" This is the best animated superhero movie I believe my kids and I have ever watched. That movie always seems to make its way into the DVD player every few weeks in our house. The creators of this movie are genius. Tons of energy, creativity and thought are put into every frame of every minute of the movie that is crammed full of so many great memorable quotes. Most important of all to me is the family theme that runs throughout the film as the producers show how each member learns his or her role in their team.

One of my favorite scenes is in the middle of the movie when Elastigirl and her kids are on the way to save their father from the evil villain. After the enemy shoots down their aircraft the mother thinking on her toes swiftly forms herself into a parachute and holds the kids as they fall into the ocean. There they are treading water and the scene continues as the mother says..

"Those were short ranged missiles, land based… that way's our best bet "she says pointing in the direction of the smoke left in the sky.

"You want to go *toward* the people that tried to kill us?" says Dash the younger sibling.

"If it means land… yes" The mother replies

"You expect us to swim there?" the daughter says sarcastically.

And the mother replies, "I *expect* you….. to trust me"
The next scene you see how they team up together to get to safety as she has formed herself into a small raft, Dash the son is holding on the back as his speedy legs are kicking to power the boat and they glide quickly across the water and the daughter is sitting on board. Sounds a bit whacky I know but I would highly encourage you to watch it. In the middle of this life-threatening situation (even though there only cartoons) they were able to work together and make something good of the situation. Their family learned how to work together through tough times and worked together to come to their father's rescue.

In all things God works for the good. That's what it says but do you believe it? How can God work for good in all things? All things can't possibly be good. If it was in any way good it wouldn't be that bad in the first place would it? Do you personally think it's possible that something horribly terrifying as personal struggle or even death itself can be turned into something good? Have you ever experienced something like that before?

I know that phrase is used a lot. "All things work out for good" especially in the Christian world. It often just seems too cliché. On September 11th I remember watching the attack of the World Trade Center. The images they showed will be forever engraved in a lot of our minds as the news played them over and over. Later that morning I got a call that Todd Beamer, a brother of one of our friends from Church, was on board the plane that was headed possibly for the White House. I went over to their house that morning and really had nothing to say. I just thought I'd try to provide some kind of comfort or at least let them know

I was there to support them. We prayed together in the doorway as she was in tears and after we finished I remember this verse coming up in conversation. "All things work together for God for those who are in the Lord." That verse instantly took on a whole new meaning but it still wasn't 100 percent clear. How was this going to be good? This was far from good. Hundreds of people had just been murdered. Families were now missing husbands, dads, moms, sisters, brothers, aunts and uncles. How is that going to turn out good? No one at the time had a good answer for that and even if they tried to explain it to me it still seemed very "cliché".

Needless to say we know how it all turned out. It was a major loss to many families, it was a major blow to the country but in the process, many people started to pray again, our nations churches started to fill back up, we as a country became a little stronger and Todd Beamer's wife, Lisa as well as her father in law have impacted many lives across the country through their story of hope in a time of despair and Lisa's book *"Lets Roll"* that well defines her and her families faith in God through it all. That is the happy ending to the story. There has been good from this event and God has been a big part of it.

The hardest part about finding good in any situation is that we often don't turn to God and discover His will for us as we deal with it all. Faith is letting go and letting God. Once you are able to do that good things really do start to happen. I personally believe that God not only has worked out some bad experiences for good but continues to do it everyday. Maybe he even will let us face those bad experiences so we can learn how He works. I know many times in my own life where I have seen God in action when dealing with situations like these and believe me it's an ongoing process as I am stretched beyond what I ever thought I could be. I love the old classic hymn Tis So sweet to trust in Jesus:

> *"Tis so sweet to trust in Jesus, Just to take Him at His word*
> *Just to Rest upon His promise. Just to know thus saith the Lord"*

He said it so it will be. We are called by God to serve him. Not to worry. He will make good out of the bad. It's a promise. It's written in blood. It's in the Bible so it has to be true. I long to just have that un-natural response to believe without cause and effect, without evidence or proof. Just to say "Ok God lets see what you got!" and know that it will happen without trying to conning myself into believing it before hand.

"I think he can, I think He can"

I've struggled long enough in circumstances by myself. It's draining, exhausting and un-bearable. I'd rather not suffer when I know someone else can deal with it and actually *wants* to take care of it for me.

God keeps saying to me, "I will take care of you, lead you out of the dark, and make it all good."

"Ok God, so great I'm just supposed to sit here and think its all going to work out?"

To which He replies "Yes. It will all be ok. I'm not asking you to understand how that will be. I'm asking you to trust me."

You can't do anything. Just let it go. Let it *all* go. Done. Gone. Over. God's in charge. Wait to see what He can do. Wait to see what He *will* do.

Deeper

> *"The hardest part about finding good in any situation is that we often don't turn to God and discover His will for us as we deal with it all. Faith is letting go and letting God. Once you are able to do that good things really do start to happen."*

1. What does it mean to "let go and let God?"

2. Do you have examples in your life where God worked a major crisis situation out for good?

3. How can our worship of him help us through a difficult time?

CHAPTER 5:

HOPE FLOATS,
SO HOLD ON TIGHT

One of the big news stories in the news this particular week is about two teenage boys who were stranded at sea for 6 days on a sailboat. You might have heard about it. It's a miraculous story of survival, rescue and hope. The two teens had set out on their small sailboat on a windy day when they noticed they were going to be in trouble with the weather and tried to head back immediately. Instead of making it back to shore they were sent out farther into the sea. For six days they struggled to survive. All tackle had been lost so there was no way to catch any fish. No food to eat, no fresh water to drink and more than 100 miles from where they began.

After six days of no food and water, trying to survive the sun and not be eaten by sharks they had no hope in being rescued. Troy, one of the two teens on the sailboat was reported saying, "I asked God to take me, You're out there fighting for your life. We didn't want to fight anymore." Hope was lost and all they wanted to do is to be removed from the situation. Take me away. I can't hold on anymore. After six days, these guys were spotted by another boat and brought to safety not too long after they had given up all hope of rescue. I could never imagine being in a place like this with no where to go and so little to try to survive with. I don't know if these teens even really know who Jesus is but it's obvious that they, as mentioned earlier in their time of need, recognized a higher power and turned to it for answers. This story goes to prove that we are wired to search and find hope, reason and significance in something more powerful and greater than ourselves. Red, black, white, young, old, tall, hairy, bald, credentialed, Democrat or Republican. No matter what, we are all naturally driven to turn towards God in all troubles and look for hope. We are wired that way by the creator. Even if it was a last resort for these guys, they felt maybe there could be some hope or resolve if they called on God. Miraculously, to their surprise, that's all it took.

Hope: True of False

Hope. Now there's a very small word that's totally misunderstood. What exactly is it? Where can I find it? Where can I get more of it? Most often when people hear the word hope it's associated with the idea of happiness or wishing. No matter how much of that kind of hope you have its guaranteed to go nowhere really fast. A great example of a false hope that many of us can relate to is those lucky digits we call the lottery. It might also be a word that comes to mind when gambling at the Casino. That would be better defined as luck or chance. Why else would thousands of people everyday stand in line at the local Circle K and spend their hard earned cash on a small piece of paper with random numbers? It's the ultimate temporary hope to win millions and then life will be perfect. It's the ultimate hope that lasts a day or two or maybe a couple weeks as you anxiously await those random numbers to be called. Stats show that in the past few years the lottery jackpot has been higher than ever and totaling hundreds of millions of dollars. People are hopeful, just in the wrong kinds of stuff.

So what do you hope for? Major weight loss? To be out of debt? New job? Better relationships? Answers to all life's problems?? Hope motivates and encourages us to look beyond the present struggles and know what lies ahead can be better. Hope is the fuel to keep the fire burning when you are completely burnt out. It's a beacon in the night when we are surrounded by the blinding darkness. It's the energy we often need to face another day when we have lost the will power to do anything more.

Hope? What's that?

Everyday everybody uses the word hope in some way or another. It is constantly running through our thoughts and conversations. Here are some you may have even used today:

- I hope you feel better
- I hope things work out
- I hope the weather is nice today
- I hope I pass this test
- I hope I get that job
- I hope

It's obvious we use the word frequently but we are still confused on what it really means. Hope according to the Merriam-Webster online dictionary is defined like this:

1: to cherish a desire or anticipation, hopes for a promotion
2:archaic: TRUST
Transitive senses
1: to desire with expectation of obtainment
2: to expect with confidence : TRUST
Synonym: see EXPECT

I think the last two transitive senses really say it all. "To desire with expectation and to expect with confidence." That is real hope. It's being completely sure there's something more than what's visible to the eye. In Hebrews it continues with that thought as it defines faith and says, "Faith is being sure of what we hope for and certain of what we do not see." Real hope is visible only through the spirit and once we have that vision we can find completeness. Hope is not only something that is helpful through the storms of life but also is a major part of our survival. It brings us motivation, encouragement and support. It encompasses so many parts of life we don't even know. Here are some things I've discovered about hope.

- Hope is a vision, it is not wishful thinking.
- Hope is the fuel that keeps us going everyday, not a quick fix to make it through
- God designed it, the world destroys it.
- True hope is not temporary but will last a lifetime
- Hope is the truth we can not see
- If you don't have it your life is going to be completely and ridiculously miserable.

Now that you have conquered the Kevin Earnst, five minute crash course on the meaning of hope, let me tell you the most important part: where you can find it. Where can I find real hope? I can I have more of it? Here's the answer. Real hope is found in worshipping God.

Hope Is On The Way

So you're saying I have to sing in order to get hope? Yes that it. Everyone must be a singer to find real hope and if your not then you might as well give it up. I'm kidding! Of course not! Worship is really not about singing at all. It's about a lifestyle. A lifestyle that trusts and centers on God. Once we center on God through our worship we encounter real hope.

One of the key words in the Bible used to describe the hunt for hope is perseverance. Persevering through the challenges and focusing on God alone in all circumstances will amazingly saturate you with overwhelming hope. I'll be honest though, Christian or not, it is nothing short of painful and frustrating. Perseverance is getting up and finishing the race when you can't even breathe anymore. It's being positive and pressing on when absolutely nothing is going your way and you can't stand it. Been there, done that, bought the T-Shirt.

It even includes worshipping God when God himself seems to absent and even when family, friends and maybe even your church has left you stranded. Been there, done that, won the trophy. No matter what the case and all sarcasm aside, God is always there in all circumstances and that fact alone you can depend on. Hope is obtainable through our worship.

When you truly trust in God in every circumstance, through any kind of weather, never letting go of that fact and centering on God alone, you will find yourself intoxicated with never ending hope. Check out these words Paul writes to the church in Rome.

> *"May the God of hope fill you with all joy and peace as you trust in Him, so that you may overflow with hope by the power of the Holy Spirit?" Romans 15:13*

Paul was a person who was fueled with hope and often times that's all he had to go on. He personally had experienced the overflowing power of hope when trusting in a God who doesn't always make him self visible.

I too have tried to depend on myself and find hope in every possible way except through God. I often find myself trying to do things on my own and over and over God will knock me off my feet until I finally get it through my gigantic metal plated noggin. I know I'm not the only one that goes through this repetitive cycle. It's something most everyone can relate to. There are a lot of other gigantic metal plated noggins out there.

A Little R & R

One evening as I was in the kitchen on my trek for the perfect snack I noticed a magnet on the fridge that made me laugh. It read, "What part of rest in me don't you understand?" I had no idea where the magnet had come from or how long it had been there but I took it as a simple message to me regarding something I had again forgotten. So this little phrase " What part of rest in Me have you forgotten? has been something I use a reminder on a daily basis. Because the one thing that has been something I use a reminder on a daily basis. Because the one thing that always brings me hope in life are the promises of God. His promises and answers provide relief and relaxation just like this magnet illustrated. One of the promises can be found in Matthew chapter 11. It reads,

"Come to me all who are weary and burdened and I will give you rest. Take my yoke upon you and learn from me, for I am gentle and humble in heart and you will find rest for your souls. For my yoke is easy and my burden is light."

If you have been treading water for a long time and trying to stay afloat you know the feeling. Jesus says here if you feel that way come to Me and I will rescue you. I will remove what weighs you down and give you rest. Why not take advantage of that? We live in a world that is overwhelmingly hopeless. In the midst of the hopelessness you can find anything and everything possible being accepted as permissible in order to find reason, peace and happiness. Real, endless hope is hard to come by and extremely rare but hope in God through continual worship to Him can bring the relief you need. False hope that the world offers so much of only brings temporary relief and brings you full circle back to looking for something more eventually. Bottom line, whether you believe it or not is, the only real lasting hope in life is found in the creator of hope itself. Why look for it anywhere else? Need a little R&R? Hopelessness got you stressed out? Drop the dead weight and run.

A Prisoner of Hope

In Romans 15:14 we find a verse that says "For everything that was written in the past was written to teach us, so that through endurance and the encouragement of the Scriptures we might have hope." There are dozens of stories in the Bible that speak of hope. It tells of people who were devastated and facing things that most of us would never even dream of dealing with. It tells of how they found hope and encouragement and made it through and ending up on top. The stories in the Bible are purposely there to give us examples of people who faced challenges, endured through them and found hope se we can learn from them and have it too.

One of my favorite people in the Bible is the apostle Paul and for the main reason that he was a rebel with a cause. No one else was put through as much torture for any longer amount of time over and over and yet still found the energy and strength to hang on. Through his experiences he was able to write and inspire people in the churches he ministered to and to people over generations facing the overwhelming disease of hopelessness. Check out his words in II Corinthians 11:26-28,

> *"I have been constantly on the move. I have been in danger from rivers, in danger from bandits, in danger from my own countrymen, in danger from Gentiles; in danger in the city, in danger in the country, in danger at sea; and in danger from false brothers. I have labored and toiled and have often gone without sleep; I have known hunger and thirst and have often gone without food; I have been cold and naked. Besides everything else, I face daily the pressure of my concern for all the churches."*

Ultimately Paul had hope in God and showed it as he worshipped Him in all circumstances even while chained up in prison. No one would have ever expected what was going to happen that night in the Philippians jail. Two men sat there worshipping the God of hope in the dark, in shackles, in a time of crisis. Hope came and set them free. Literally.

Hope in Bloom

Ok, you've heard all the hope info, now its time to actually try it out. What do you have to lose anyway? Go ahead and hope in something bigger than you ever could imagine. Hope in the creator of hope itself. With a little never ending hope in something big you will find it soon will become a part of your identity. It's the fuel that the human heart needs to continue beating. It's the lifeline that the spirit needs to thrive. John Ortberg writes in his book, "Living the God Life" writes. "A car crash or a diving accident can paralyze the body, but the death of hope paralyzes the spirit. " It's true. It can literally bring life to your spirit.

I have seen over and over how true hope comes to full bloom through personal worship. Not only does worship develop hope but it also can become an addiction as you draw close to God in worship and he keeps filling you up with a positive spirit and outlook on everything. It erases the doubt and confusion. Hope will saturate your spirit when you develop a closer walk with God. It will leave you desperate to come back for more. The present may look dark and creepy but somehow you will have joy knowing it won't last forever. What God has in store will be more than fulfilling. It's going to be good. There are guarantees. Hope the world offers will always cycle back around to disappointment. Hope in things that are eternal brings nothing but complete satisfaction.

Reality Check

Reality Check. Let me make a little disclaimer here. First of all, even though hope may bring joy, having hope does not equal the absence of problems. (Sorry to burst your bubble. I just thought you should know that before you got all excited.) It's a way through the problems, not a way to get rid of them. That's often a hard thing to grasp. Second, complete hope doesn't happen instantaneously. It's a process.

"While we wait for the blessed hope—the glorious appearing of our great God and Savior, Jesus Christ, who gave himself for us to redeem us from all wickedness and to purify for himself a people that are his very own, eager to do what is good."

Waiting is a pain. We live in a fast paced world. Waiting is not cool. God does not live in a fast paced world and waits on us all the time. Wait on God to bring you the complete hope. Trust Him and let it slowly sink in. Practice perseverance. Perseverance and hope open doors to something greater that we can't see.

Confessionals

Have you ever felt like you have totally disappeared from God's radar? You've prayed the prayers and waited for days, weeks or months but still struggle to see the hope in it all? Even though you know it has to be there somewhere? Like maybe you were deleted from His friend list on Facebook.com or something. (No, God doesn't have a Facebook page, I already looked but that would be pretty cool.) Let me be completely honest. I have been a Christian for over twenty five years, a pastor for over ten years and always involved in the church in some way or another since the day I was born. In all those years I admit I have lost hope maybe once or twice. Ok maybe 5. Alright, alright. It happens all the time. Why? Because I too am enticed into searching for hope in all the things that are temporary just as we all are. No I'm not admitting I'm a lottery addict or that I doubt God. I just get hit hard with personal struggles as much as anyone while I continue in the lifelong process of putting complete hope in God. It's not easy. If it is for you then you have an awesome spiritual gift. Whatever the case, I know my hope today is stronger than it ever was. The problems still come, and the pain seems to never end when you are feeling overwhelmed and not finding results but through the perseverance I find my hope is blooming.

"Let us fix our eyes on Jesus, the author and perfector of our faith, who for the joy set before him endured the cross, scorning its shame, and sat down at the right hand of the throne of God. Consider Him who endured such opposition from sinful men, so that you will not grow weary and lose heart." Hebrews 12:1-3

Carved in Stone

The news story I wrote about at the beginning of this chapter talked of hope lost after struggling to survive and never seeing any sign of rescue. Another major news story just hit the air that again reminds me of what hope is really all about. It's the un-believable school shooting nightmare in the Amish community of Georgetown, Pennsylvania. Just when you thought you had literally seen it all you are again shocked to find out you haven't. MSNBC's website news title on the story read *"Amazing Grace, Amid Devastation"*. I watched the online clip and keep playing part of it over and over in my head as Ann Cury briefly interviews one of the men.

Ann: *"You say you've buried your anger before even burying your own children. Have you already forgiven? How is this possible?"*
His simple reply, *"With God's help."*
You know this guy is suffering greatly from his loss. It's written in the expression all over his face. But what you can see even more is that he honestly offers forgiveness to the shooter and his family and has a hope in something greater. Something greater than all the present crisis that unfolded. What a great witness to the world as this story is broadcasted through the media and the web as he lives out the words Paul wrote to the Hebrews.

"Let us hold unswervingly to the hope we
profess, for he who promised is faithful"

Sinking Deeper

You're on a journey to completion. All the circumstances you encounter will make it clearer. They won't however always make it easier. God knows exactly what is coming up around the corner. That alone you can find hope in.

PLAN A

"For I know the plans I have for you" declares
the Lord, plans to prosper you and not harm
you." Plans to give you a hope and a future."

Jeremiah 29:11

Plan A is the original plan. The plan we often find ourselves steering away from whether intentionally or unconsciously. The plan God had in mind for you way before you were born and before the world began. You might be asking "So life has a plan? There is order to this? I have a destiny? Is there anyway I could maybe see what it is?" Take a look at your calendar and you can see what day of the month it is. Take a look at your day timer, your palm pilot or your blackberry and you can see what you have scheduled for next week. Or even next month. What's on your schedule? It's easy to keep track of events that we plan and are involved in regularly. When it comes to the plans for your life and future that's a whole different story. Everyday seems to bring a new twist to your already made schedule of tasks and responsibilities. Every now and then it gets more complicated as major changes occur and leave you stranded changing all your plans for months to come. What then?

Speaking of plans, I remember my junior year of high school being asked what I am going to do as a career. "What are you going to do now? Where are you going to college?" I would just stand

121

there looking deeply confused. I had no idea. I was just trying to live one day at a time and make it through high school. That's enough pressure in itself. Come my senior semester I still didn't have plans really although God did as he used others around me to encourage me and direct me to attend college to go into music ministry. Almost five years later I graduated and people started asking again, "so what are you going to do now?" I still had no idea. Don't get me wrong I did have some goals and ambitions but I really didn't know where I was to be used. Any graduate can tell you there are a lot off pressures to know what your plans are. "What's next? Where are you moving to? What are you going to do? What are God's plans for you?" Funny thing is you can often ask many forty year olds the same question. Often times you will get the same answer. "I have no idea."

Some of life is plan-able. The rest seems to plan you. It always seems when things are "going as planned" that's when change steps in and reorganizes. Throughout this book we have looked at many aspects of going through unwanted change and heartache and how to deal with it. What makes it hard is trying to figure out what God has in store. Ok I am learning to handle the stress and the pain but what's the plan? Where do I go from here? Plan A doesn't seem to be working. (the way you want it to anyway) Plan B completely fell through. Plan C is nowhere near accomplishable now. What do I do? One day you think God is opening doors and answering your prayers and the next you're not so sure. There is nothing like living life feeling unsure of what tomorrow holds and having no idea what you are going to spend your life focusing on. It is very hard when you're confused on the direction of your life and have big decision to make. After all you've had to make plans and decisions before and look where those got you.

Notice that nowhere in this verse does it say, "You know the plans I have for you." It simply "I know the plans (referring to God of course). We don't know what God has in store but He does and most likely he keeps the full detailed description of the plan to himself so we don't end up screwing them up somehow. It also doesn't say "plans to make you totally miserable and in a state of utter confusion for the rest of your life", but "plans to prosper you and not to harm you." That's what I want to hear. His plans are to "give you a hope and a future". It's not over. Hope is on the way. The future is bright when God is in charge.

Not too long go on a very beautiful sunny day I went into the dining room where my kids were eating breakfast and asked, "Ok guys I have some plans and ideas for us to do today. Do you know what they are?"

"No, tell us, what!" They said and their eyes lit up.

"Do you really want to know?" I asked again.

"Yeah tell us!" You could feel the excitement building.

They were excited about what was in store even though they had no idea what the idea was at all. In the same way you don't have to know what the plans are. Just be hopeful. Stick with plan A and know that you are in for a big surprise. It already says right there that they are going to be good so there's no reason to worry. Sooner or later he's going to let you know what's next. Even if you have to wait a little longer. (or more than you want to) God always has good plans. We just need to know that when it comes to scheduling next week or next month, in all reality we aren't really in charge. All is subject to change. Don't worry, don't fret, and don't lose heart. Be hopeful. Be hopeful through all the waiting. Be hopeful through the struggle. Hope is the lifeline. God's big un-veiling of the plans will be soon. Pray, wait and listen. As you trust in God you will hear those words you have been waiting to hear.

"Hey guys, I have some plans and great ideas for you. Do you want to know what they are?" Are you ready for what it is? Take out that sentence and add in…

I guarantee it will be worth the wait and more exciting than you could ever imagine!

Deeper

> *"There is nothing like living life feeling unsure of what tomorrow holds and having no idea what you are going to spend your life focusing on. It is very hard when you're confused on the direction of your life and have big decision to make. After-all you've had to make plans and decisions before and look where those got you."*

1. Do you have any plans for your life?

2. Do you think these are the same plans God has for you?

3. How can you use your life plans to worship God and follow His will?

PERMANENTLY STUCK

" For I am convinced that neither death nor life, neither angels nor demons, neither the present nor the future nor any powers, neither height nor depth nor anything else in all creation will be able to separate us from the love of God that is in Christ Jesus our Lord."

Romans 8:38-39

I hate superglue. I know its powerful stuff so I don't even use it. Powerful glue scares me. I am often klutzy. Superglue and klutzy don't go together. One time while trying to fix a toy I glued my index finger to my thumb. At first I thought it was permanent. I tried every solution possible to get it to dissolve. No luck. So now instead of having five fingers on my right hand, I had three individual ones and one big round one that was connected to my hand at both ends. This makes it very hard to do everyday kinds of things such as shave, write, play an instrument, type and so on.

Superglue really works. When I was a kid I remember seeing a commercial for superglue. (Hopefully someone else reading this will remember this commercial too.) It showed this guy wearing a hat that was glued to his head and then the hat was glued to a long steel bar which was hanging him out over empty space very high on a high rise. I was convinced at the time by what I saw as a kid and all my doubts of this actually working were erased.

There is no doubt that it could hold in this fashion although it would be very painful and very stupid. Even though I do believe to this day it could hold a man up leaving him dangling several feet above the ground I still have my doubts that someone was actually dumb enough to superglue a hat to their head, superglue the hat to a bar and demonstrate the miracle of this product for the sake of a commercial. This would definitely be the ultimate example of a stupid human trick.

Almost two days later my fingers were still stuck. By this time I had developed all new habits and procedures to carry out my day without having any difficulty. I wasn't going to go to the emergency room for something embarrassing like this so I thought I'd manage on my own. I typed with my three fingers, I tried learning how to be ambidextrous (let alone spell ambidextrous) and often when I waved it just looked like I was giving them the OK sign. All was well. It was a pain but I dealt with it. Then not too long after I had developed these new skills it finally loosened and wore off. I was then back to five fingers again.

A lot of times we find ourselves hopeless and maybe even feeling worthless as we go through seasons of difficulty. It's too much to bear and handle and before you know it you lose all motivation. I was reading in my Bible one day and ran across this verse at the beginning of this story that stood out like a sore thumb. I read it again and again. Before I knew it, it began to give me hope in a whole new way. Here's why. It says that there is nothing, nothing at all can separate us from the love of God. Absolutely nothing. Life, death, forces of evil, power, your past, any measurable distance, a crow bar, a giant wedge. Not anything in the world. God loves us no matter what and we are never separated from Him.

If there is anything that is for sure in life it is that difficulties and problems will always come your way. Everything changes. But the one thing we can know for sure as worshippers is that nothing can separate us from the love of God. That is something to hold on to. It's actually the only thing you can hold on to.

Through even worship itself we can find ourselves sticking closer to God. When going through any crisis if we understand that God still loves us then it's easy to understand that there is hope. If nothing can separate us from God's love then why would we want to try to separate ourselves from it? Especially when we can't? When facing a difficult time it's easy to just say I can't take it anymore and give up. What can bring hope though is that God is still there and his love will never give up. It brings stability in a time of insecurity. It brings hope in a time of despair.

Even something as powerful as superglue will eventually wear off. The love of God endures forever. Nothing can stop it. Nothing can separate us from it. That to me brings hope beyond measure. It sticks around through all kinds of weather and never fades. As you probably know by now there are some pretty strong forces in the world that can create division. You see it happen in our communities, our churches and in our homes even in close life long relationships. Sometimes they are things that we have control of and sometimes things we don't have control of or can't even see. Paul in this scripture explains to the church that God has made us more than conquerors and part of that power is the one true fact that God is always with us and on our side.

No matter what comes our way, no matter how you feel, no matter if you try to separate yourself from Him or His love, His connection with you will always be stronger than superglue. This kind of love in a world like ours is exactly what we need to hold us together and keep us from breaking to pieces. The human idea of love and God's idea of love are quite a strange combination. With love like His you are stuck together forever. It's powerful stuff and brings hope for anyone who knows it. It's everlasting and it's stuck all over you. It's not coming off.

Deeper

"Absolutely nothing. Life, death, forces of evil, power, your past, any measurable distance, a crow bar, a giant wedge. Not anything in the world. God loves us no matter what and we are never separated from Him."

1. What do you think it would be like to be separated from God?

2. What kinds of thoughts come to mind when you hear that God is always with you no matter what?

3. Ok I have to know. Have you ever seen this superglue commercial before?

OUT OF THE BLUE

"Why So downcast O my soul? Why so disturbed within me? Put your hope in God, for I will yet praise Him, My Savior and my God."

Psalm 42:5

Both of my two sons Corey & Ethan over the years have developed a huge interest in music. They have guitars, a little toy keyboard, congas, recorders, they write songs and sing quite often around the house. I have no idea where they get it from. What is really cool is when they write songs. Sometimes they rhyme. Sometimes not even close. Sometimes I have no idea what they are talking about and others I find stuck in my head for weeks. One night after I came home from the evening services they had setup a mini concert for me of some songs they wrote. Here is one called God and even though it is awesome it made me laugh so hard I started choking violently.

God
One day a Savior was born then he had a head of thorns.
And said he'd be back someday, I wish that day was today.
Last time He was on earth it was his birth
For 33 years till everyone was in tears
Now we have Sears and He's still not here's
Come on God can you please come soon
Maybe before noon before the guitars out of tune.

I tried not to laugh, or to choke. It was great. It really was. It just caught me out of the blue and I lost it. (Call me evil or heartless but I still think the song is hilarious… in a good way of course) A few years ago I remember a song Corey sang. Ethan played the drums. I was just playing my guitar and he breaks out into a big blues riff crying out randomly throughout the song as I accompanied him. Here's a sample verse:

"We don't have cable anymore, I've got the blues.
Can't afford cable anymore, I've got the blues.
No more SpongeBob or Scooby Doo and I don't know what to do
I've got the blues."

Music is a powerful tool used to express yourself in many different ways. Blues music obviously as we know is a way to vent sad feeling, a way to express yourself while being down on your luck. This song again even though a blues number brought me to tears laughing as well as the rest of the family as we entertained each other. (and anyone else in a half mile radius around our house)

The Psalms are full of "blues" music as David sings of his troubles and heartache. This guy had quite a few tough things to sing about. He had been swept away many times by disaster and crisis but never gave up on his two biggest passions, his music and his God. Through his songs he was able to express himself and worship even while angry and depressed.

In the middle of the song he wrote here in Psalm 42 he just stops and asks himself. "Why am I so depressed? What is up with that? Why do I feel so down and miserable? This self appraisal hits home as David gives us a perfect example of something we need to ask ourselves at times. Are you ever depressed? Feeling down? Why do you think that is? Could it be maybe because you have lost your focus and put your hope in things that are completely hope less? He then comes right out with a personal reminder to himself to simply "put your hope in God!" What else is there really to be hopeful about?

In Psalm 42 David sings about an interesting chapter in his life as he reminisces back to the days he was a worship leader in the temple. He thinks of the privilege it was just to lead the congregations or multitudes into the throne room of God in song and praise. This is something I can relate to 100% because I have the great honor to lead others into the presence of God in many different settings for over 10 years now. Here as David wades through those thoughts and through all his pain he has endured, he not only remembers those moments but also that he can find joy and hope in God as he continually praises the Lord. In similar words he states, no matter what I may feel, I will find hope in God as I yet praise Him through the hurt.

Music itself can help soothe the soul and bring comfort. It can stir up old memories or emotions. It can also help you vent what's on your heart and mind. It has been scientifically and medically proven to help reduce clinical depression and is often used as part of treatment for similar disorders. Music is unique that way. Music was created by God.

Even while singing the blues in this chapter David finds comfort as he vents his feelings and worships the Lord at the same time. That is why musical worship is so awesome and important. It has power. As the songs flow from our hearts and our mouths we begin to focus on God and find healing. As we draw near to Him everything in life seems to slowly fade away and we find ourselves feeling new and restored. It brings peace and builds hope. It helps us to connect with God and see Him for how great He is. There is power in music. There is restoration in worship. If you have not experienced that yet you have not experienced true worship.

I love music and listen to it all day long. When I experience worship though there is no doubt that as I sing my heart out to the Savior all the pain I may have had before is erased and I begin to see things from a new perspective. You can find hope through worship. You can find endless hope in the One you worship. Worship allows you to express yourself to Him. A creation enjoying the creator. It also fills you with all you need to find motivation, happiness, satisfaction and peace. For so long you have been troubled by the trials that come your way. Why not take advantage of the opportunity to bring your heart back to life. Worship in song, even if you can't carry a tune in your pocket. Worship and focus on the only true source of hope and healing. Sing and make your thoughts known to the Lord. Shout, cry dance, laugh and sing praise. Sing for joy, sing the blues, you will find hope and be filled with laughter again. You will be made new and be rescued from your gloom. Worship Him in the morning. Worship Him in the evening. Worship Him all the time in between. Worship Him when you're happy and when you are depressed. Worship him with your life. Worship brings hope. Put your hope in God and as you worship everyday He will fill you with more and more hope until you begin to overflow and all your blues have turned to praise.

Deeper

> *"Music itself can help soothe the soul and bring comfort. It can stir up old memories or emotions. It can also help you vent what's on your heart and mind. It has been scientifically and medically proven to help reduce clinical depression and is often used as part of treatment for similar disorders. Music is unique that way. Music was created by God. "*

1. Do you worship God in song on a regular basis? Or if you can't sing do you listen to Worship type music?

2. What is one of your favorite worship songs? Why is it your favorite?

3. How has music been a tool for you to connect with God?

HOPE-FULL

"Those who hope in the Lord will renew their strength. They will soar on wings like eagles. They will run and not grow weary; they will walk and not faint."

Isaiah 40:31

I don't know about you but everyday my email account seems to get slammed with dozens of pharmaceutical drug ads that overflow my inbox. Everything from pills to give you a better focus all day long to the infamous drug we all know as Viagra. No matter how strange it might be or funny to think about Viagra is a hot commodity. Just two years ago you would have never heard of anything like it and now it's a common household word and medication. It's proven to work, it's affordable and so everyone in need can take advantage of this wonder drug and be promised results.

Over the years the medical and pharmaceutical world has boomed coming up with pills, vitamins and other remedies to solve almost every problem and meet almost every need. Or so it seems. Why are there so many different pills? Because there are so many different physical and mental problems. One of the main problems or conditions of society today that there is no real medication for is the disease we all know as hopelessness. The world is overwhelmed with hopelessness and has no clue where to find the cure. Too many negative things going on in life bring a ton of hopelessness. Struggle after struggle and endless pain leads to restlessness, stress, fatigue and the biggest killer of all, depression. Before you know it you have no will to carry on and not to mention any motivation whatsoever. That's where the real wonder drug needs to come in. Think about it! Who wouldn't jump at a solution like that! I'm not talking about alcohol, illegal drugs or a quick chocolate fix. I'm talking about a miracle drug that provided something as powerful as hope. The problem is drugs (legal and illegal) only provide temporary relief. That's why they come in bottles and prescriptions. When you run out you just get some more.

Hope amazingly has several similarities to prescriptions. It doesn't come in bottles but it does come and go. It can boost your energy level but also can leave you feeling empty. (If you have been fed with a false hope) Real hope as everyone knows is hard to come by and very hard to hold on to. The key is knowing where to find hope that really works. This verse says it all in the first few words.

"They who hope in the Lord will renew their strength.

Hope in the Lord. No pre-cautions. No disclaimers or negative side effects. Hope in the Lord –strength renewed. It isn't temporary but it will leave you desperate for more. Hope in God is what brings ultimate strength. All other remedies are temporary fixes. No doctor can prescribe that kind of quick & permanent solution.

I remember as a kid reading this verse and memorizing it for Sunday school. It always seemed extremely weird to me.

"They will soar on wings like eagles. They will run and not grow weary, they will walk and not faint."

For some reason I always just pictured a guy out in his Nikes and jogging shorts with giant wings stretching out from his back as he swiftly ran down the side of the road without a hint of any fatigue or being winded. What did it really mean though? I now understand it a little better. It means that a person with hope who hopes and waits on God in all situations will find strength, will be renewed and not feel overwhelmed with the pressure to give up or give in. To be honest that's a feeling I've had a lot and can relate to. The feeling of giving up or just saying I've had enough and just moving on to something new. There is only so much you can take before you feel like your going to break or snap.

What's the point of so much pressure and pain? Is there a real reason for it? God doesn't want you to have to deal with so much pain but you better believe God is going to take advantage of the circumstance to make a better you of it all. So when you feel you are at the end and have lost all hope, when you have taken all you can take before going off the deep end its time to stop and realize where is God taking me here? How strong is my hope in His plan? Why do you feel the way you do? It's simply because you have put your hope in the wrong place. Instead of hoping in the Lord you have put hope in yourself and are trying to take care of life your way. If hope is in God you will have strength. It will bring you peace and direction and as the prophet Isaiah writes it will give you the boost of energy you have been looking for and will never fade away. The real trick is learning how to let go of those feelings of hopelessness and depression and finding strength in the creator.

I imagine when Viagra was first discovered those who first experienced it were eager to share this new scientific breakthrough with the world. And why not when this new wonder drug would not only solve the age old problem of impotency but also rake in a huge profit for those who discovered it. Who wouldn't want to take advantage of a drug like this?! You are probably wondering why in the world I would choose to use an illustration like Viagra in these thoughts on hopefulness. To be honest I have no idea but I know for a fact that if Viagra can bring so much hope to those in need and take the pharmaceutical market by storm, just think of how much more hope in the Lord can bring endless strength and renewal to your life! Think how it could turn your miserable life upside down. It's just a thought I had. Something to think about the next time you too get an email box full of those wonderful medical advertisements.

Deeper

"Hope in the Lord. No pre-cautions. No disclaimers or negative side effects. Hope in the Lord –strength renewed. It isn't temporary but it will leave you desperate for more. Hope in God is what brings ultimate strength. All other remedies are temporary fixes."

1. What kinds of thoughts come to mind when you read this verse in Isaiah?

2. Do you ever find yourself leaning towards the temporary fixes to permanent problems?

3. How does worship of the creator a remedy for your hopelessness?

THE BOTTOM LINE

Never be lacking in zeal but keep your spiritual fervor serving the Lord. Be joyful in hope, patient in affliction, faith-full in prayer."

Romans 12:12

I like simple. Skip the detailed mumbo jumbo description. Forget the full analysis and give me the final answer.

"What it all boils down to is…"

"The bottom line is…."

That's what I want to hear. Everything in between is pointless and forgotten. However even though I am all about the bottom line answer or response I somehow often find myself being the mumbo jumbo distributor that I despise. This usually happens most when I am getting after my kids. If you're a parent you know what I'm talking about. You spend 20 minutes regurgitating the same old info repeatedly until your blood pressure is ready to max out meanwhile they have already clocked out after your first couple words.

In Romans 12 you can find a handful of cut to the chase, bottom line statements that speak volumes when searching for ultimate hope and peace. Are you ready for it? Here it is. Short and to the point. Three simple instructions.

> *"Be joyful in hope, patient in affliction, and faithful in prayer."*

That's it. No long paragraph or extensive detail. Just three simple things. By doing this we find ourselves focusing on God through the challenges and actually worshipping Him. After all as I already said, worship of our God is the ultimate remedy for complete peace and hope.

At first all of these statements look like a list of ridiculous and impossible ideas. Joyful in hope? Why be patient in pain? If only these steps were as easy to complete as they are to read. Take the first one for example. Joyful in hope. What did he actually mean by that? When struggling through a hard time sometimes the only thing that can pull you through is just a little ounce of hope. Paul is saying that real hope will bring happiness no matter what the situation is. If we actually find hope that brings joy we are fully trusting God and in return we are worshipping Him through our action. Rejoice in the hope given and you will find continual joy. Bottom line, being joyful in hope means complete trust in God, letting go of all worries and fears and knowing the best is yet to come.

Then there's that phrase "patient in affliction" which is a pretty amazing thought. Normally when you're in pain the last thing you want is to be patient. Why be patient you're your in misery? What could possibly be the benefit of that? Does God want us to when in pain just deal with it and suffer? Absolutely not. But there is a major lesson to learn in the suffering. For in the suffering we get to see God in action. Being patient and waiting on God even when in pain can bring awesome results. It brings us slowly in tune with his plan and helps us realize that we are not in control and actually can put us in our place as we wait and watch. It sounds strange but somehow that's how God can get through to us the best. If you have ever watched the popular television show 24 you are familiar with Jack Bauer's tactics on how to get the terrorists to talk. He induces pain. Whatever the method may be his goal is to get results. He means business. Jack could do amazingly painful things even with a number two pencil and a ball of yarn. The bottom line is pain. Even though unwanted and often un-tolerable proves over and over in the end result to bring amazing benefits when trusting in the will of God. Take for example the outcome of the cross.

Out of all the statements in this short verse this last one seems to be the most easily to comprehend. Faithful in prayer. That's the easiest one of all. Who doesn't pray to God repeatedly when facing problems? Or I should say... Why aren't we praying to God when we face problems? When Paul mentions the word faithful after writing the other two steps referring to patience, endurance and perseverance I think he is saying to pray even if you don't hear answers in a day or two, a week or two or even a month or two. Remain faithful in prayer ever week, every month and continually find yourself in prayer no matter how long it takes to get results and even if you never get any at all. That you may see anyway.

Three simple steps. Be joyful in hope, patience in affliction, and faithful in prayer. Even those all can be summed up in two simple words. The bottom line is..... Trust God.

Deeper

> *"Be joyful in hope, patient in affliction, and faithful in prayer."*
>
> *That's it. No long paragraph or extensive detail. Just three simple things. By doing this we find ourselves focusing on God through the challenges and actually worshipping Him.*

1. How would you define being joyful in Hope?

2. Have you ever found patience in affliction?

3. Do you have a faithful prayer life? Take a moment and pray over these three things

CHAPTER 6:

ELEVATION REVELATION

I love going to the beach. It's one of the most relaxing beautiful places you can find to get away and soak up the sun. Growing up in Michigan I can remember all the summer days and other seasonal times we spent at many different beaches along Lake Michigan with friends and relatives. Yes, believe it or not there are hot summer days and beautiful beaches along the west side of Michigan that are very breathtaking. I can remember camping, exploring along the shoreline, climbing the sand dunes, swimming, jumping the waves and many endless exciting adventures.

On a clear day on Lake Michigan if you hike up the enormous dunes the wind has formed off the water you can look across the southwest corner and see small figures, like tiny fingers, sticking out of the water. Even though it's hard to make out, those "tiny fingers" happen to be the skyline of one of America's favorite cities. Has any idea what city it might be? You probably guessed it already. It's Chicago. Now of course you can't see across every large body of water in the world, like Lake Michigan but this view from point to point is literally over 118 miles! That's pretty amazing! This view, seen by the naked eye, puts a whole new perspective on the world.

You can physically see what's out there and what's beyond your present location. It's a small piece of the bigger picture.

What's on the Other Side?

It would be awesome to be able to see life like that. Just climb to the top of the hill or mountain and get a higher perspective on the road that lies ahead. What's on the other side of this mess? Where am I headed? What's next? What's the plan? I don't know how many times I have said this already in this book but… if we could only get a glimpse of what's behind the present issues that cloud our daily life each day it just might make things so much simpler. Or so we think. Present complications would seem easier if we knew what the outcome is on the other side. I wonder if that's what helped fuel the passion of Jesus as he endured the endless torture and his ultimate death on the cross. Salvation for the entire world, talk about a great motivational factor. Then again there is nothing easy about death let alone death by crucifixion. Nothing compares to a love like that. Hindsight makes things clearer and puts everything into perspective. Looking forward through whatever obstacles stand in your way takes complete faith and sacrifice.

You could not find a better resource for understanding this principle than the life-stories in the Bible. I believe God had that in mind when he carefully chose each of the life-stories included in the scripture. It is literally packed through and through with regular people in this same situation. Every single one of them had some gigantic, painful challenges to deal with before they were able to find their part in the ultimate plan and even while fulfilling their God-given calling. Each one of them struggled through pretty significant events and kept their eye on the goal as God stretched them into something more.

Take a look:
- Moses was sent to the desert for 40 years to wait on God's calling
- King David faced spiritual warfare and depression and even while in his leadership role

- Esther struggled with finding God's direction for her life while placed in the kingdom as a queen.
- Job (you know the story)
- Jesus spent 30 years in preparation, 40 days in a desert, over 12 hours on a cross
- Paul never stopped being tortured.

Take a closer look at Joseph for example. As the youngest of many brothers, Joseph often got the shaft but was shown favoritism by his loving father. Joseph knew in his heart he was chosen by God to do great things with his life. God had a major plan for him yet he had no idea what it could be. Or when it would be. He often was discouraged and wondered if this was ever going to come true as life continually day after day sent him wandering down another mysterious path.

Joseph had been given a dream of this great plan God had for Him and his brothers began to disown him because of it. This was just the beginning. They eventually sold him into slavery in Egypt, later, his master's wife falsely accused him of trying to rape her, and, as a result, Joseph was thrown into prison. This guy had one bad situation after another following him wherever he went. When was it going to end? Was there really a plan or was this something he had made up in his head? What was on the other side of these disturbing and challenging events? What was the point? Why was this happening to him? What had he done to deserve all this? Better yet, when would he get his big break?

Through all the curve balls thrown his way Joseph kept trying his best and achieved many great things. Even though God didn't seem to be giving him any great opportunities or escape from the torment he kept on doing what he knew was right. He kept his focus on God Finally, literally years later, it all started to turn around while he was in prison. It was there God blessed Him with the gift of interpretation and he was able to explain the dreams of key people in the kingdom. Including Potiphar himself. His interpretation of the dreams led to his knowledge of the upcoming famine and what needed to be done to prepare.

Through this one miraculous opportunity he was soon released and stepped into the role that he had been shaped for his entire life. He became the right hand man and was entrusted with the welfare of the entire country. God used him right where he was. Even though he was enslaved and imprisoned against his will for doing nothing criminal, he continued to grow in those surroundings and a became a vessel that God could use in a mighty way. The time had come and the door opened. He finally got his big break that he well deserved.

God took his situation and location and turned it all into something more than Joseph or anyone could ever imagine. The same guy who had just minutes before was taking up space in a prison cell was now a powerful leader overseeing Egypt's entire agriculture department! Why did he have to endure several years of change, challenge and torment? Why did this have to happen to someone who was on fire to be near the heart of God? It was all part of the plan and as he sought after God in all circumstances his life-story was written exactly as God wanted it to be. For Joseph, even though he had been through major changes and struggles he saw the bigger picture. The story has an amazing dramatic ending as later he was reconnected with his brothers as they came to him, not knowing who he was in their time of need. He didn't get angry, show bitterness or have them executed. Instead he overflowed with joy and forgiveness as he explained how God has used them and every situation for good. What a powerful story.

Life by the Book

So what's your story? It might not be understandable from where you are standing but God does have an ultimate plan. God watched Joseph go deeper into a relationship with Him through the entire crisis that came his way. God had involvement in his life the whole time through thick and thin. Everything was planned & timed precisely so his efforts and endurance would be rewarded as he landed in a role he never expected. To me that story gives hope and deeper meaning to all the challenges that come our way.

What if I told you that I believe that the present crisis struggle and heartache you might be facing has been uniquely engineered and arranged for you for your own benefit? I know that sounds very existential. The first time I heard that thought I gave the person a pretty dirty look. Really though. I'm not saying someone has put a curse on you or is looking to make you miserable for their own good. I am saying someone has taken your current life circumstance and has carefully planned out a detailed, organized map of how it will all work out. It's God. That's what He does. He's got you right where he wants you for the time being even though it may sting a little or be intensely painful.

Whatever the case, if you don't believe me just wait and see. If I had a dollar though for all the times I've heard people say "God doesn't want to cause grief and heartache but only wants to use crisis situations to help make you stronger" I would be able to retire. It's a quick and easy reply to the question "why do good people have to face so many bad situations?" But honestly I'll be the first to say it hardly ever brings any relief. Although true the real idea is that every life event, situation, problem, crisis, etc is a smaller piece of the giant picture. No matter how you look at it.

Think of it this way. God provides the place and the characters for the story with a guaranteed ultimate happy ending that we can choose. The story unfolds as we make choices and decisions in whatever drama comes our way. It's up to us to choose what route to take but to our advantage we have two things that can guide us. The script (Bible) and our own personal coach (the holy spirit). It is our job to keep worshipping God through whatever hell comes our way. Even though our story is written perfectly we often change the plot making it a little more intense or even stepping it up to the Rated "R" category. Sometimes we complicate it more than we ever needed to just because our limited perspective and own personal egos lead to confusion and unwise decisions. You may think, "Well of course we can see how Joseph's life-story turned out good because it's all written down already." You don't even have to read the whole thing. You can just skip ahead to the ending and see how it all turns out.

Our story on the other hand, is still being written. It's still fresh on the drawing table. So how do we know what to do and what route to take? Let's back up. Here's the easy answer. The script is there to follow. It's already been written by God. As a matter of fact He knows your whole personal, detailed story. He's watched it several times, seen the reruns and bought the DVD. He knows how it will turn out and offers to coach and prompt you along the way to get to where we need to go. Not sure what route to take? Stick with the script. If we keep our focus on that we will reach our full potential and have a life with a have a happy ending.

An Arizona point of View

It's kind of ironic that I started writing this last chapter about water and the whole idea of loving to go to the beach when I presently live in Arizona. Water obviously is not a high commodity here and especially in Northern Arizona where I now live. We have lakes here (or giant ponds, or at least big holes where water used to be) but they are nothing like the ocean or the lakes of Michigan. However, just like the view from the top of the dunes I mentioned at the beginning of this chapter there are many places in Arizona where you can literally see for miles. In the high peaks and mountains in northern Arizona you can look out and often see hundreds of miles away. The mountains look a short distance away but really are about 2-3 hours in drive time. It's really pretty amazing. The land is so open you can see the road ahead as far as you could imagine. The peaks stand out like small silhouettes in the distant sky. When it does rain you can see the rain clouds coming way before they even reach your area. At night the stars shine bright and hang so close you swear you could reach up and grab one. The view is amazingly captivating.

It's like an enormous panoramic picture both day and night as the open sky allows so much visibility and the heights provide scenic overlooks of all over the state.

I often find myself being reminded through the scenery here that I need to take a bigger look at what's going on in my life. I need to try and take in a whole new point of view when things get rough. Even though it may seem cloudy in your life with no way out, from God's view of things you have nothing to worry about. The rain clouds don't cover the whole area. (You can see them actually passing by from on top of the mountain and it's actually still sunny not too far away from here.) As hard as it may seem if we simply allow ourselves to let God do the piloting and we just take the directions we will end up right where we need to be every time. As we ultimately rely on God in all circumstances no matter what the struggle or how miserable it is we will better understand how all our circumstances fit together. If we keep worshipping Him for all He is we will never lose sight of the other side.

One helpful thing to keep in mind is that if you are intently chasing after Jesus and continually find yourself running into another wall, you are definitely headed in the right direction. Why would I say that? It's very simple. Because if we are passionately chasing after God we are going to run into dead ends. We are going to be mis-directed. It's part of the package. The bad guy in the storyline doesn't want you to reach the ultimate ending or your life-story to be published. God however will come meet us where we are and help us to keep our eyes on the goal, the main reason for life itself.

Not too long ago I saw someone had written in their Facebook status, "...wants to go to a place far, far away". Everyone feels that way at times and when thinking about that I wrote a song which has become my favorite called "There's a Place". These words were written to help me and everyone who hears it remember where to find peace in the midst of chaos and where I can go to escape. A few weeks after I wrote this song I had the awesome opportunity to go hiking here in Flagstaff up the San Francisco Peaks to a place called Lockett Meadow. This place is one of the most beautiful places I've ever been as Ponderosa pines tower over the trails and the mountains are like backdrops as you climb to the top of this path and see the view. It is a place where you can go to get a way, to see things from a "higher perspective" and find sanctuary with God and his creation. Suddenly this song came to life as I had found the place I had been writing about. Here are the lyrics.

There's A Place
There's a place I know that's far away from here
Far away from here,
Where I can go
To escape from all the voices in my head
And things that I've not said
And the questions

It's a place I often find I'm dreaming of
When I have had enough
And need you more
And it's there in the beauty of that place
That I can see your face
Everywhere

Chorus:
You are there with me, You are there
And I run into your arms
You are there with me
You are there

There's a place that puts a smile on my face
Every second of the day
And I have no fear
For every moment there my spirit is renewed
As only you can do
Only You

Chorus:
You are there with me, You are there
And I run into your arms
You are there with me
You are there

And its there you're love's surrounding me
I can see You here, I know you're near
You fill me with a peace that's comforting
And you speak to me, You say to me

Chorus 2:
I am here for you, I am here
Come and run into my arms
I am here for you, I am here, come to me

There's a place I know that's far away from here, Far away
from here

The Worship Factor

Here's the bottom line. The key to get a higher perspective on everything is one simple thing. It doesn't have to involve climbing a mountain or even being physically elevated. It is simply possible through the power of our worship.

One of my favorite authors Tommy Tenney has a great book out on this topic called "God's Eye View, Worshipping Your Way To A Higher Perspective." Take a close look at four powerful statements he makes in this book regarding the power of worship.

- "The power of a higher perspective is accessed through worship. Worship will lift your spirit. Worship will change your destiny. Worship will re-arrange your future."

151

- Worship possesses the power to make the problems you face seem small while magnifying other things.
- "Worship is the greatest of all mood altering drugs. It possesses the power to turn your darkest night into your brightest day. Worship will loose the winds of heaven to lift you on wings of praise into God's presence. Depression, discouragement, grief and sorrow, they pale in power and influence when you begin to praise God.
- Worship is all you need to get to the prearranged intersection, the divine rendezvous of revelation where God waits to speak destiny into your soul and unveil His provision for your pain.

It might sound completely crazy or sci-fi first but it does work. Worship your way into his presence and all of your struggles literally disappear. Have you ever noticed how when you're having a bad day if you focus on helping someone else in a tough time it seems to bring some relief to your own present burdens? That's exactly what is being said here. If we completely surrender to God and worship him from the bottom of our hearts when we are facing hardships we will be lifted from the water and will not drown in despair.

Advantages of Drowning (Metaphorically Speaking)

No, I'm not encouraging drowning. Not literally anyway. But imagine what it would be like if you could completely empty yourself of yourself and fill up the enormous void with the spirit of Jesus. Kind of like the way water enters fills up your lungs and fills the void in your body. Complete surrender to God and abandonment of self. It's hard to imagine. It's hard to do. No one wants to turn themselves over and be taken control of. It sounds cultish. Giving your whole life to God? That doesn't seem fair! After all it's your life right?

Not so much. It isn't. We were created by God to worship Him. As a matter of fact we were actually created worshipping from day one! We in our lifetime have found ways to replace that worship towards God with other forms of worship that satisfies self. We have tried to re-wire ourselves to please self instead of showing worth to God. We have been steered away from our focus and now it's haunting us. This is where all the pain, heartache and struggles begin to set in.

Remember that symbol you learned in grade school? It looked like this > . Sure it looked simple but it symbolizes what is greater and what is less. 100 is greater than 10 (100>10). Try this. Use this symbol to remind yourself God is greater and you are less. (God>Me) More of God, less of me In John 3:30 we an actually find scriptural reference for this.

"He must increase and I must decrease."

He must increase. I must decrease. The only way to do that is to worship. Empty yourself and fill the void with God. Less of me, more of Him. This will help you put life into focus again. This will bring you back to real worship that we were created to do. This will help to erase all the struggles in your life and give you a higher, clearer perspective on what's coming your way. Sink deep into worship and you will be filled with a new passion for life.

Going Deeper

So life threw you an unexpected curveball. The questions start flooding through your mind and you feel like you're drowning in a sea of hurt, pain and confusion.

Keep praying
Keep waiting
Keep hoping
Keep persevering
Keep Worshipping

You may not have any idea why you are at the place you are in your life presently and why you have to go through what you're going through. The opportunity however has arrived for you to go deeper into the heart of God and to know him more personally. That's an opportunity you need to take. If you think what your facing now is big and overwhelming remember this, it has no comparison with the joy, the awesomeness and the breath taking wonder of what is on the other side. The best is yet to come.

I have personally experienced this and that's why I spent all this time trying journaling all these thoughts down so I could share it as a personal testimony and encourage anyone in the same position. God is fully in control and if we give our focus in worship to Him everything starts slowly to make complete sense. Throughout the book you have seen the acrostic I included for the word worship. After many months I finally wrote this out and put it on my bathroom mirror as a daily reminder. These are ways to worship without singing or using music. These are steps to develop a worship lifestyle. These are ways to worship God in the storm. They may seem basic but they are important and not as easy as they may seem. Each one involves letting go of yourself completely and filling up with God. Remember this acrostic:

Wait on God, (welcome to your new hobby)
Openly ask for help (cry, scream, yell, whatever it takes)
Realize you are not in control, (Sorry, its true)
Surrender your plan for a better one, (Give it all up)
Hope in God (There is a way out!)
Imitate the lifestyle of Jesus (What better role model could you ask for?)
Praise him continually (In the good, the bad and the ugly)

These things altogether make up a passionate lifestyle of worship and will move you closer into a relationship with our compassionate God. Believe me the view from there is incredible!

Worship through the storm.
Worship when the waves come crashing in.
Worship when you feel like your drowning. . .
It's all about the ***worship!***
Worship will take you deeper into heart of God who has
phenomenal purpose for your life. Worship Him for that and
see what will happen.
It's time to sink a little deeper.

NOTES

Chapter 1

1. Max Lucado, Come Thirsty (Nashville; Publishing Group/ Thomas Nelson, 2004)

Chapter 2

1. Bob Laurent mentioned in this chapter is a professor at Bethel College and a great teacher. I heard him speak at Granger Community Church in Granger, Indiana several different times in their Midweek service. You can download some awesome messages from him on I-tunes and I would highly encourage that.
2. Matt Redman, The Un-Quenchable Worshipper (Ventura, CA; Regal Books, 2001)

Chapter 3

1. Tommy Tenney, God's Eye View, Worshipping Your Way To A Higher Perspective (Nashville; Thomas Nelson, 2002)
2. Rick Warren, Purpose Driven Life (Grand Rapids; Zondervan Publishing,2002)
3. Quote from "The Count of Monte Cristo" (If you haven't seen this movie yet when you are done reading this book, go rent it)
4. Quote from Yoda (Do I really need to include a Bibliography for this?)

Chapter 4

1. M. G. Easton, Easton Bible Dictionary (New York: Cosimo, 2005)
2. "Sweet Love" from the CD Heaven Help Me Released Kevin Earnst © Overflow Music 2001 ASCAP
3. Quote from the movie "The Incredibles" , Another awesome movie you have to see!

Chapter 5

1. Mirriam Webster online dictionary; http://www.merriam-webster.com/
2. John Ortberg, Living the God life (Grand Rapids; Zondervan, 2004)
3. MSNBC website story; http://www.msnbc.msn.com/id/1510530 5/?GT1=8618

Chapter 6

1. Tommy Tenney, God's Eye View, Worshipping Your Way To A Higher Perspective (Nashville; Thomas Nelson, 2002)
2. "There's a Place" from the CD "One Step Closer" released in July of 09 Kevin Earnst / Overflow Music ©2009 ASCAP

ABOUT THE AUTHOR

Kevin is a musician, songwriter and worship leader living in northern Arizona. He is currently finishing his third CD and this is his first book. He has been a leader in the indie music world with a variety of musical styles ranging from modern rock to acoustic style worship. His music has not only been published for worship use but also been given airplay in the U. S and over 5 other countries. His music has impacted people of all ages over the years in many different settings from the church, to conferences and concert venues in the mid-west and now in the southwest are of the country where he now resides.

"Everyday I find myself using creativity, whether journaling, photography, songwriting, blogging or video to express the unique experiences and things that God brings my way. If you get wrapped up in the awesomeness of God in your everyday life it's hard to contain and inspires to create and capture as the Creator designed us to do. Using these forms of art we've been given we can find ourselves worshipping in a whole new way, in all situations and sharing with others more about our awesome God. "

For speaking engagements or more information on using this book as a sermon series at your church visit the website listed below.

Kevin's third and new CD release, "One Step Closer" will be available Summer '09

Check out Kevin's blog, photography and music at:

www.Kevinearnst.com

Made in the USA
San Bernardino, CA
08 June 2018